THE LITTLE BOOK OF

FAMILY HISTORY

Written by **Chris Mason**

THE LITTLE BOOK OF

FAMILY HISTORY

This edition first published in the UK in 2007
By Green Umbrella Publishing

www.gupublishing.co.uk

Publishers Jules Gammond & Vanessa Gardner

Printed and Bound in China

ISBN: 978-1-906635-89-3

Contents

Introduction

Why do people want to start delving into the history of their own family? It's probably got a lot to do with wanting to know why we are the way we are and where certain traits in our own character come from. Whatever the reason, almost everyone who investigates their family tree soon finds that the whole business, while it can at times be a little frustrating, is nevertheless extremely fascinating. Many people do not start to take an interest in their roots until they are getting on in years but, increasingly, younger people – many of whom naturally have access to computers – are also becoming involved.

Whether you are young, old, or somewhere in between, if you are considering investigating your family history, then the best advice is to make a start as soon as possible. Your ageing relatives will not live forever and if you don't ask them questions about their childhood and their own parents and grandparents, their memories are likely to die with them. Most of us have regrets about not asking enough questions before it became too late.

Of course, people have always been interested in the history of their own families and have always asked questions of their relatives.

In times past however, more detailed research was not all that easy. For one thing, the material was often widely scattered and not easy to locate. For another, so-called 'ordinary people' had neither the time, the money, nor perhaps the education to delve very deeply into the life and times of their ancestors. Many people knew, or believed they knew, about their antecedents, but family history was largely a matter of oral tradition, with stories handed down from generation to generation. In some communities this is, of course, still the case.

Further research could normally only be undertaken by those with the time and financial resources to undertake it. Elderly vicars from 'good families' might spend years trawling through the various records and they often had old family papers to help them. While those middle or upper class amateur genealogists often did sterling work, they tended to look only on the bright side of their families. Every family has its 'black sheep' – people who refuse to conform to the moral climate of the

ABOVE A Victorian family at leisure

LEFT Several generations of a family on their way to church

day – but the perceived dirty deeds of the black sheep were largely ignored by earlier generations of family historians. They preferred instead to concentrate on those who had toed the line and maintained the honour of the family, followed their forebears into one of the respectable professions, or generally bettered themselves.

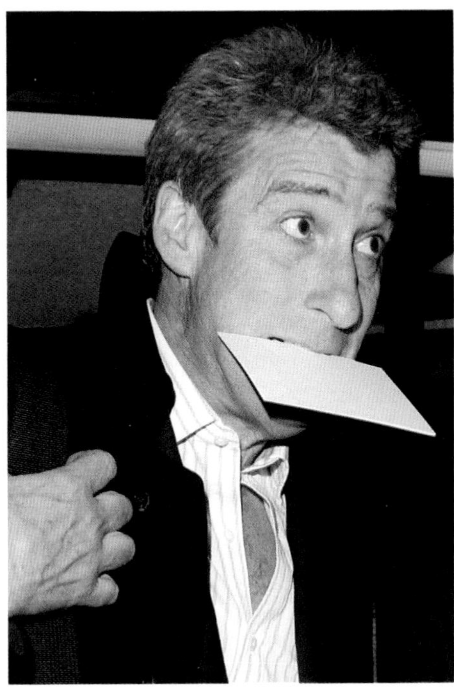

Early family historians would sometimes behave like historians in the former Soviet Union, by either completely ignoring someone's existence, or by simply making a vague passing reference to them. Women who gave birth out of wedlock would be subjected to such treatment as, during their lifetime, they would have been very much despised. Such women were considered to be 'no good' or 'a bad lot' and their offspring would be ignored by the rest of the family. Mind you, if a young gentleman got a household servant 'into trouble' that was deemed rather more acceptable. More acceptable, perhaps, but not to be written or talked about.

Things are of course very different today. Attitudes have largely changed and, with far more resources available to everyone, researching the history of one's family is a lot easier. It is no longer the exclusive province of the middle classes or the idle rich and most of us will be more than happy to discover the previous existence of the odd black sheep or 'fallen woman'. Research can however still be very time-consuming and you will, from time to time, come up against a brick wall. A lot will depend on just how much time you have available and on how far back you wish to go. When you start out, however, you will probably make quite a bit of progress in a fairly short period.

ABOVE Jeremy Paxman featured in the popular BBC2 series

LEFT A parson with members of the congregation

The hobby of tracing one's family history has increased in popularity to a quite

ABOVE Stephen Fry who took part in the BBC series ' Who Do You Think You Are '

remarkable extent in recent years. This increased popularity is reflected in the amount of television time now devoted to the subject. Family history seems to be taking over from gardening, cooking, moving house and buying and selling antiques and collectibles. Our so-called 'celebrities' are now in on the act and their reactions to finding out about their ancestors can be quite fascinating. Early in 2006, in the B.B.C. series Who Do You Think You Are? notorious softie Jeremy Paxman was almost reduced to tears on learning about the poverty and deprivation suffered by some of his forebears. When asked at the beginning of the programme if he was excited by the thought of delving into his family's past, he had replied that it was a stupid question; of course he wasn't excited. Interested, yes – but not excited. He seemed to feel differently half an hour or so later.

If only we all had a team of researchers employed by the B.B.C. to do the work for us. On the other hand, that would take a lot of the fun out of it. Sorry, Mr. Paxman, but as you now know, it really can be fun as well as, at times, emotionally exhausting. Many of us will find that we have paupers, rogues and even outright criminals in our family tree. Most of us won't find members of the aristocracy hanging from a lofty branch, but we are all likely to discover people from more than one social class amongst our ancestors and it is this mix of people, their living conditions and their occupations, which can make it all so fascinating. As Stephen Fry said in another edition of Who Do You Think You Are? "It makes you realise how intimately interwoven with history we are".

There is an amazing amount of archive material relating to individuals of the past. The trick is to know how and where to find it. Much information is now available in computerised form and access to a computer will help significantly – although primary sources should always be checked, as computerised records are prone to errors. It is of course perfectly possible to investigate your family history without the aid of a computer. Record offices still have large numbers of hand-written and typed documents: it will take years to computerise everything and some of it may never be done.

The purpose of this book is to act as a starting point for family history research. It does not pretend to be a comprehensive guide, but it does hopefully contain enough information to set you on your way. Towards the end you will find lists of addresses and websites referred to in the text.

ABOVE Beards were very popular a hundred years ago

Good luck with your investigations!

Getting Started

The first rule when researching your family history is to start with your most recent ancestors and then work backwards. If there is a family rumour that your father is descended from, say, the Duke of Clarence, don't start trying to trace the descendants of the illustrious Duke in the hope that your research will lead to Dad being able to claim his rightful inheritance. It almost never works and will probably be a total waste of time.

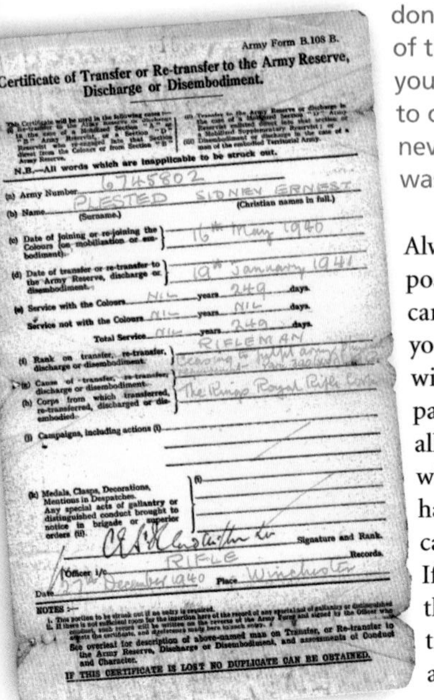

Army Form B.108 B.

Certificate of Transfer or Re-transfer to the Army Reserve, Discharge or Disembodiment.

N.B.—All words which are inapplicable to be struck out.

(a) Army Number 6745802

(b) Name PLESTED (Surname) SIDNEY ERNEST (Christian names in full.)

(c) Date of joining or re-joining the Colours (on mobilization or embodiment). 16th May 1940

(d) Date of transfer or re-transfer to the Army Reserve, discharge or disembodiment. 19th January 1941

(e) Service with the Colours NIL years 249 days.

Service not with the Colours NIL years NIL days.

Total Service NIL years 249 days.

(f) Rank on transfer, re-transfer, discharge or disembodiment. RIFLEMAN

(g) Cause of transfer, re-transfer, discharge or disembodiment.

(h) Corps from which transferred, re-transferred, discharged or disembodied. The Kings Royal Rifle Corps

(j) Campaigns, including actions (i)

(k) Medals, Clasps, Decorations, Mentions in Despatches. Any special acts of gallantry or distinguished conduct brought to notice in brigade or superior orders (ii). (i)

Signature and Rank.

RIFLE Records.

Officer i/c

Date 27th December 1940 Place Winchester

NOTES :—

i. This portion to be struck out if no entry is required.

See overleaf for description of above-named man on Transfer, or Re-transfer to the Army Reserve, Discharge or Disembodiment, and assessments of Conduct and Character.

IF THIS CERTIFICATE IS LOST NO DUPLICATE CAN BE OBTAINED.

Always begin by assembling as much data as possible from your living relatives. If you can, get them all together, tell them what you are doing and, with luck, the memories will come flooding back. Parents, grandparents, aunts, uncles and even cousins are all likely to have useful information which will get you started. Your relatives may well have copies of birth and marriage certificates and even death certificates for those who have left this world. If they don't know exact dates, ask them roughly when, for example, they think someone was born or died, as this will save you a lot of time later. Record or write down everything they tell you: it will not always be accurate but you can check it out later.

Once people start to think over events of the past, they often come

up with things that had been long forgotten. It is therefore a good idea to discuss their recollections with your relatives more than once. Indeed, it's a good idea to keep going back to them – provided you don't make too much of a nuisance of yourself! And while you're at it, get them to check in the loft for any forgotten family items. You never know what they might come up with.

Most older relatives have stories to tell about their ancestors. Even though they may not be totally accurate, they will very often have more than a grain of truth in them. As an example, the author's mother was convinced that her uncle was brutally murdered on a tea plantation, probably in Ceylon (Sri Lanka) sometime during the 1890s. It turned out that he was indeed brutally murdered – whilst on a hunting trip in East Africa in 1907. He had nothing to do with tea plantations and was in fact a cable-laying engineer, working on a ship moored off Mombassa.

It is a sad truth that some older people are ashamed of their origins, particularly

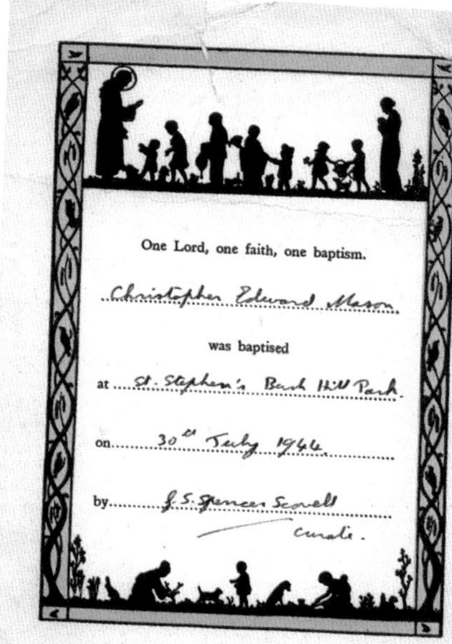

One Lord, one faith, one baptism.

Christopher Edward Mason

was baptised

at St. Stephen's Bush Hill Park

on 30th July 1944

by J. S. Spencer Scovell
Curate.

ABOVE Baptismal Certificate

MIDDLE Public Record Office, 50 years ago

LEFT Army Discharge Form

if they come from a poor background and you may find that some of your older relatives are reluctant to tell you too much about, for example, their own parents. Even in the recent past, attitudes towards divorce and illegitimacy were very different from those of today. A story which is regarded as a skeleton in the cupboard by your aged grandparent may be no more than an interesting fact to yourself, but you may need to tread carefully to elicit the truth. Once you have done so, you will then need to check the facts.

If you are extremely fortunate, you may have paintings or sketches of your

BELOW John Lennon and Yoko Ono's marriage certificate

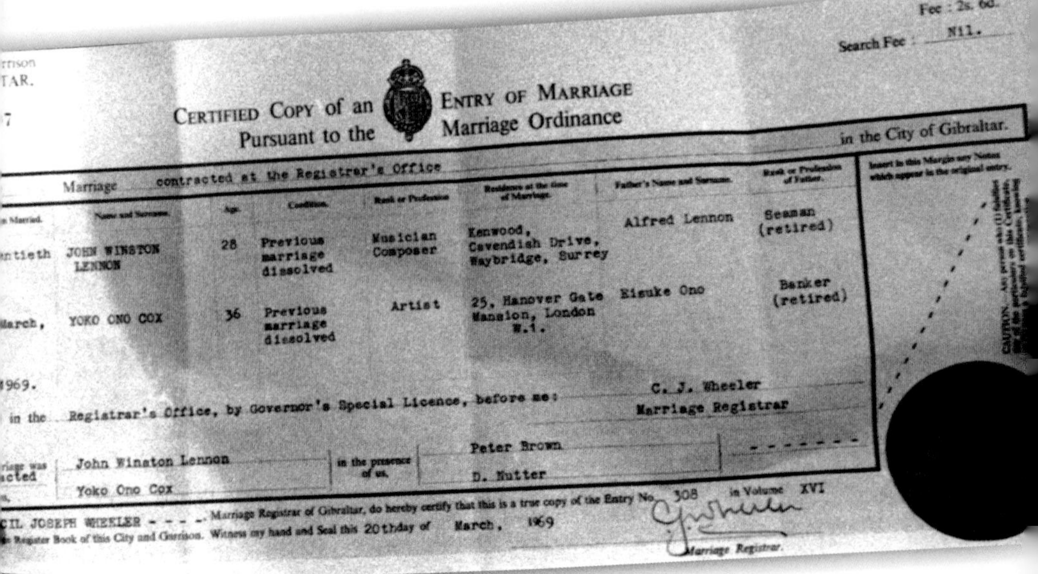

Fee : 2s. 6d.
Search Fee : Nil.

CERTIFIED COPY of an ENTRY OF MARRIAGE
Pursuant to the Marriage Ordinance

in the City of Gibraltar.

Marriage contracted at the Registrar's Office

Name and Surname	Age	Condition	Rank or Profession	Residence at the time of Marriage	Father's Name and Surname	Rank or Profession of Father
JOHN WINSTON LENNON	28	Previous marriage dissolved	Musician Composer	Kenwood, Cavendish Drive, Waybridge, Surrey	Alfred Lennon	Seaman (retired)
YOKO ONO COX	36	Previous marriage dissolved	Artist	25, Hanover Gate Mansion, London W.1.	Eisuke Ono	Banker (retired)

1969.

in the Registrar's Office, by Governor's Special Licence, before me: C. J. Wheeler Marriage Registrar

John Winston Lennon
Yoko Ono Cox
in the presence of us, Peter Brown
D. Nutter

CIL JOSEPH WHEELER - - - - Marriage Registrar of Gibraltar, do hereby certify that this is a true copy of the Entry No. 308 in Volume XVI
Register Book of this City and Garrison. Witness my hand and Seal this 20thday of March, 1969

Marriage Registrar.

ancestors – and, if you are yet more fortunate still, you'll know just who they are. For most people however, the only pictorial depictions of their ancestors will come in the form of photographs. Photography got going in the middle of the nineteenth century and by the 1870s portrait photos really began to come into their own. Apart from forming an important part of your family history in their own right, such photographs can be a very significant source of information. They sometimes bear names and dates, although this is by no means always the case. Someone once came across a photograph on the back of which was written 'This photograph was taken a long time ago'. Very helpful!

ABOVE Domestic staff from a Victorian household

If you are not sure which ancestor is featured in the picture, it may be possible to get an idea of the date from the style of clothing worn. The photograph may also give you some kind of indication as to the likely wealth, or otherwise, of the person or persons pictured. Beware though – in days gone by, very poor people would save up to have their photo taken and would be sure to wear their 'Sunday Best' for the occasion.

You may have some old family photographs yourself, but be unsure of the identities of some or all of the people pictured. A hundred years ago, middle-aged people tended to look a lot older than they do today, so don't be surprised to discover that the little old lady in the picture who seems to be in her late eighties was only about 64. Always show your old photos to your older relatives, as they may be able to identify them, or the photo may bring back some of those long-forgotten memories.

Incidentally, when showing relatives old photographs, it's generally a good idea not to pass comment on the appearance of the people depicted in them. For example, if you are trying to get Granny to identify a fierce-looking elderly woman, don't say: "I wouldn't like to meet her on a dark night". The picture might be of Granny's favourite Aunt Ethel, who was actually a kindly soul and would

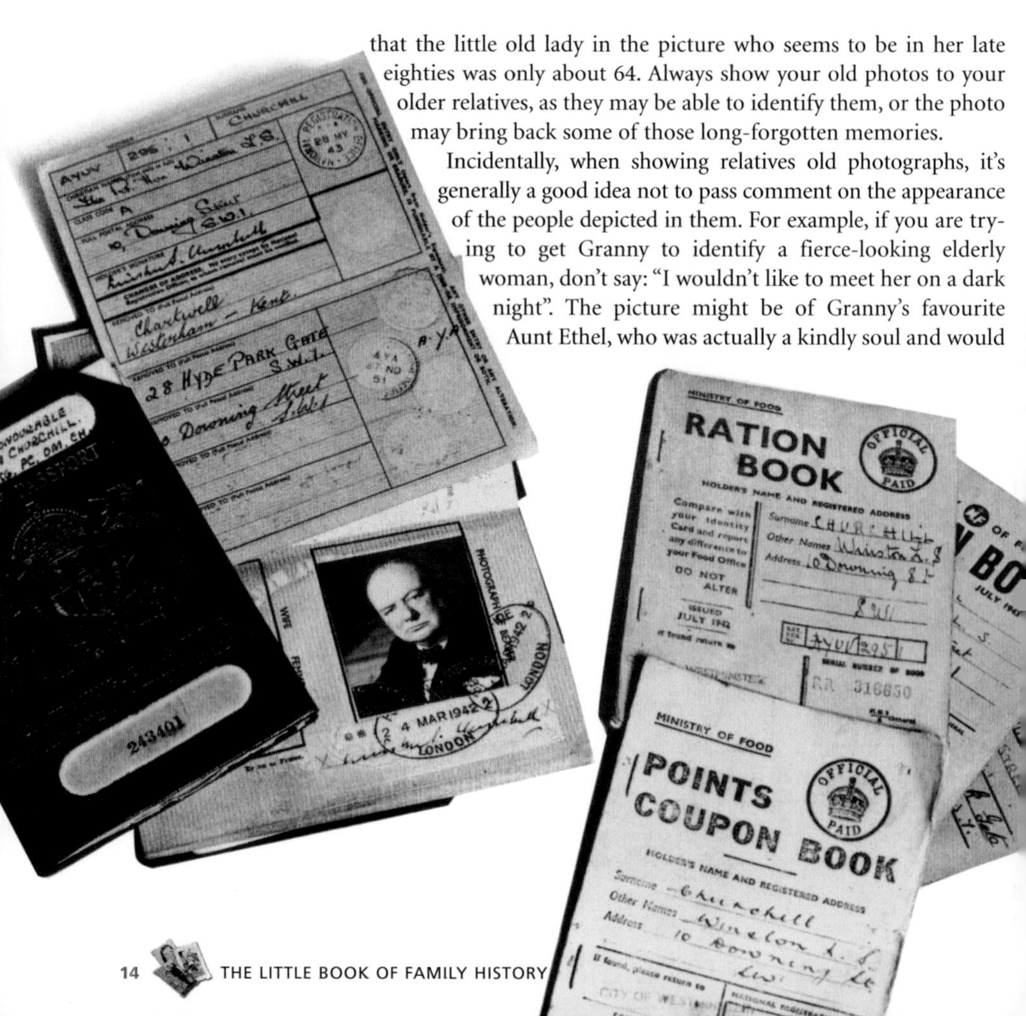

not have harmed anyone.

Whilst on the subject of photographs, don't forget to ensure that your own digitally produced recent family photographs are named and dated. Your descendants will thank you for it in a hundred years' time.

Parents and grandparents may have old school reports, qualification certificates, newspaper cuttings, letters, diaries, personal military records and medals, wartime identity cards, ration books, memorial cards and even bills for funerals – if nothing else, such bills will show you just how much the cost of dying has increased over the years. More importantly, however, a memorial card or an undertaker's bill will tell you where someone may be buried and this might lead to finding a headstone bearing more information. If your relations are reluctant to part with documents, persuade them to allow you to photocopy or photograph them.

ABOVE A ration book of clothing coupons

LEFT War time documents

Family Bibles can be a source of important information. These were often passed from mother to daughter and in some cases may be at least a couple of hundred years old. They are often very interesting in themselves, but you may well find

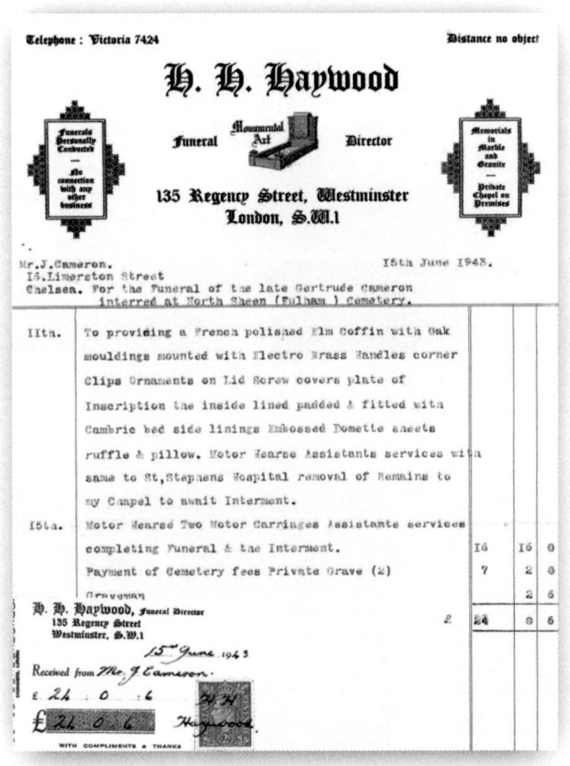

Telephone : Victoria 7424 — Distance no object

H. H. Haywood

Funerals Personally Conducted — No connection with any other business

Funeral — Monumental Art — Director

Memorials in Marble and Granite — Private Chapel on Premises

135 Regency Street, Westminster
London, S.W.1

Mr.J.Cameron. — I5th June I943.
I6.Limerston Street
Chelsea. For the Funeral of the late Gertrude Cameron
interred at North Sheen (Fulham) Cemetery.

		£	s	d
IIth.	To providing a French polished Elm Coffin with Oak mouldings mounted with Electro Brass Handles corner Clips Ornaments on Lid Screw covers plate of Inscription the inside lined padded & fitted with Cambric bed side linings Embossed Domette sheets ruffle & pillow. Motor Hearse Assistants services with same to St,Stephens Hospital removal of Remains to my Chapel to await Interment.			
I5th.	Motor Hearse Two Motor Carriages Assistants services completing Funeral & the Interment.	I6	I6	0
	Payment of Cemetery fees Private Grave (2)	7	2	0
	Graveman		2	6
	£	24	0	6

H. H. Haywood, Funeral Director
135 Regency Street
Westminster, S.W.1

15th June 1943
Received from Mr. J. Cameron.
£ 24 : 0 : 6
£24. 0. 6 H.H. Haywood.
WITH COMPLIMENTS & THANKS

ABOVE Undertakers bill from 1943

RIGHT Football programme seller from over 50 years ago

details of births, marriages and even deaths carefully and lovingly written in them. Such information could be invaluable in your quest.

Even items as apparently irrelevant as old football programmes may give you information. Was Great Granddad really a Fulham supporter in the 'twenties? He was born in Lancashire and he died in Yorkshire, but was he perhaps living and working in south-west London for a time? (NB: Old football programmes may be surprisingly valuable – never throw anything away!)

Some of your more recent ancestors may themselves have had a go at constructing a family tree or pedigree, or even writing up their family history. There seems to have been quite a vogue for doing this in the early part of the twentieth century and it's surprising how much information some people were able to gather. As has already been stated, research resources were much more limited at that time. Any documentation you unearth will need careful checking, as the assumptions made by Great Aunt Ada all those years ago may well be flawed.

There are, of course, various ways in which to catalogue your early findings. A simple card index may be a good idea, especially while you are still at an early stage. If you have a computer you can type up your notes and amend them later. It is also a good idea to begin constructing charts and pedigrees early on and to start writing mini biographies of your ancestors. Again, a computer will be very useful, as you will easily be able to update the biographies as you discover more information. Computer programmes are available to help you create family trees or charts, but they inevitably restrict the amount of information you can put in. You may well do better to draw up your own charts, deciding for yourself what you want to include.

The lives of our ancestors are much more interesting and indeed more understandable, when we know something about the era in which they lived. It is therefore a good idea to borrow a few books from your local library so that you can, for example, read up on life in Victorian times. Things were very different then, of course. The poor really were poor and they often had large families to bring up. There was little in the way of entertainment for the working classes

ABOVE British military medals

OPPOSITE A member of the landed gentry looking at sheep grazing on his farm

and anyway they probably couldn't afford to indulge in anything on offer. 'Demon Drink' was relatively cheap and there was always sex. It's hardly surprising families were so large.

You may well find that your family's fortunes waxed and waned over time. The landed gentry had everything going for them for hundreds of years, but by the beginning of the nineteenth century many were beginning to fall on hard times. This was partly due to depressed prices for agricultural products, following the Napoleonic Wars. So, it is not uncommon to find that a mid-nineteenth century carpenter or farm labourer had ancestors who owned land and would have been described as 'gentry'.

During the same period a new middle class of industrialists, engineers and entrepreneurs of all kinds was emerging; the sons and grandsons of the poor were in some cases becoming rich and were able to build great mansions for their families to live in. Then, quite often, their own sons and grandsons would prove to be less hard-working – and the family fortunes would be back where they had started.

Some people employ professional researchers to aid them in the search for their ancestors. There are a lot of them about these days and they certainly know their way around the hundreds of resources which are now

ABOVE A family in Victorian times

ABOVE The entrance to Somerset House, London. 1972

available. Researching your family history can, however, develop into a fairly expensive hobby (or obsession!) and the employment of professionals may add significantly to the expense. They should perhaps be put on hold until you have done a fair bit for yourself and perhaps come up against one of those brick walls. Professionals may then come into their own, by quickly solving a problem which would have taken you weeks to resolve.

Unless you get really stuck, it's much more fun to do it yourself. The staff at record offices and other institutions are usually very helpful and can often put you on the right track. If you do consider employing a professional researcher, then make sure he or she is well qualified to do the job. A list of members of the Association of Genealogists and Researchers in Archives is available from the Society of Genealogists.

An example of a mini-biography:

Name: Edith Elsie Heyward (Edie)
Born: Croydon, Surrey 28th September 1883
Died: Wandsworth 23rd March 1924

Daughter of Thomas Henry and Susan Theresa Heyward [nee Churchouse]
Half-Aunt of Doris Isabel Mason [nee London] (Dot)
Half Great Aunt of Christopher Edward Mason (Chris)

Edie was the youngest of the Heywards, born when Theresa was about 45 years old. She worked as housekeeper to the Misses Alice (Mary Alice) and Minnie (Minnie Frances) Webber, who ran the Devonshire Laundry Company at 67 Alderbrook Road, Balham. The laundry appears in Kelly's Directory for 1924 and the Webber sisters appear on the register of electors during the early 1920s. Dot is certain that Edie "lived in" but she does not appear on the register. Number 67 Alderbrook Road was a house with a laundry at the back and seemed to specialise in laundering for the Gentry.

Unmarried Edie, who seems to have been remarkably unworldly, became pregnant - perhaps by the laundry deliveryman - when she was forty years old. She died having the baby, in March 1924 and is buried in the same cemetery as her mother. The baby, who was called Philip, also died although, as his death is registered in the second quarter of 1924, he presumably survived for days, weeks or perhaps even months. The family was told that Philip had been adopted.

Births, Marriages and Deaths

RIGHT A wartime wedding

Since 1837

As previously mentioned, it is important to begin the search for your ancestors by starting with the more recent ones. Having found out all you can from talking to people and from assembling all the more recent memories, documents and photographs, it will be time to start searching the records. If your more recent ancestors came from the British Isles, then you're in luck, as centralised Civil Registration of births, marriages and deaths has been a legal requirement in England and Wales since the beginning of the reign of Queen Victoria - almost 170 years ago. It was introduced a little later in Scotland (1855) and Ireland (1864).

There were many reasons for the imposition of centralised registration. Prior to 1837, the government held little in the way of statistics relating to the population and it clearly decided that it wished to know a lot more. There were, after all, taxes to be levied and wars to be fought – for which large numbers of young men were needed. Increasing industrialisation also meant that there was more and more demand for

labour and the factory and mill owners would need to know they had a sufficient supply of men, women and children to ensure their profits continued to roll in.

LEFT A Victorian group looking at stereoscopic photographs in the parlour

From July 1837, the country was therefore divided into registration districts and sub-districts, each under the control of a registrar who reported to the Registrar General at the General Register Office. Details were recorded in registers and sent to London. Local parishes did continue to record baptisms, marriages and burials after 1837 (see below) but the centralised system has survived, with very few changes, into the twenty-first century.

The provision of official copies of birth, marriage and death certificates since 1837 means that you should be able to find documentation relating to several generations of your family. So, organise a filing system for these certificates. You are bound to need one, especially if you eventually obtain copies of the certificates relating to the siblings of, for example, your great grandparents. You may think when you start out that these 'sideshoots' are not especially interesting or important, but sometimes they can be – and once you're bitten by the genealogical bug, it is amazing to what lengths you will go in order to trace the family of Great Uncle Arthur! In any case, although it may not be possible to trace them all, everyone has four grandparents, eight great grandparents and 16 great great-grandparents. If, in time, you are able to trace a great x 10 grandparent, then he or she will be one of a total of 2,052!

Although Civil Registration was a legal requirement from July 1837 few, if any, penalties for non-registration were imposed in the early years. For this reason,

LEFT A young Victorian couple exchange wedding rings in the sight of their bridesmaids and a clergyman

quite a few births were not registered during the first few years of the new arrangements. The vast majority of poor people (and there were an awful lot of poor people in Victorian times) were illiterate, or at best semi-literate and perhaps had difficulty in understanding the new rules. In addition, there was probably an aversion to what was seen as government interference in their private lives.

Early marriages and deaths fared better, but in many ways it is remarkable that so many people did, in fact, comply with the law – especially as some members of the clergy were against the new system. Congregations generally respected the opinions of churchmen and mostly did what their Vicar told them to do. In 1875 it became the responsibility of parents to make sure their children were registered and in the same year severe penalties were introduced for non-compliance.

Even after 1875, however, the odd birth seems to have escaped registration – especially if, as so often happened, the child failed to survive. Most couples were more than happy to have their marriage recorded so you should, with perseverance, be able to trace almost all post-1837 marriages. The registration of a death was hard to avoid, so if you fail to find the record of someone's demise it may be that the person emigrated: A lot of people left British shores for the Americas and the Antipodes during the latter part of the nineteenth century and the earlier part of the twentieth. You may be able to trace records of marriages and deaths in the United States and in the colonies, but they might be harder to find.

Before 1837

Prior to the middle of 1837, details of baptisms, marriages and burials were largely recorded by the Church of

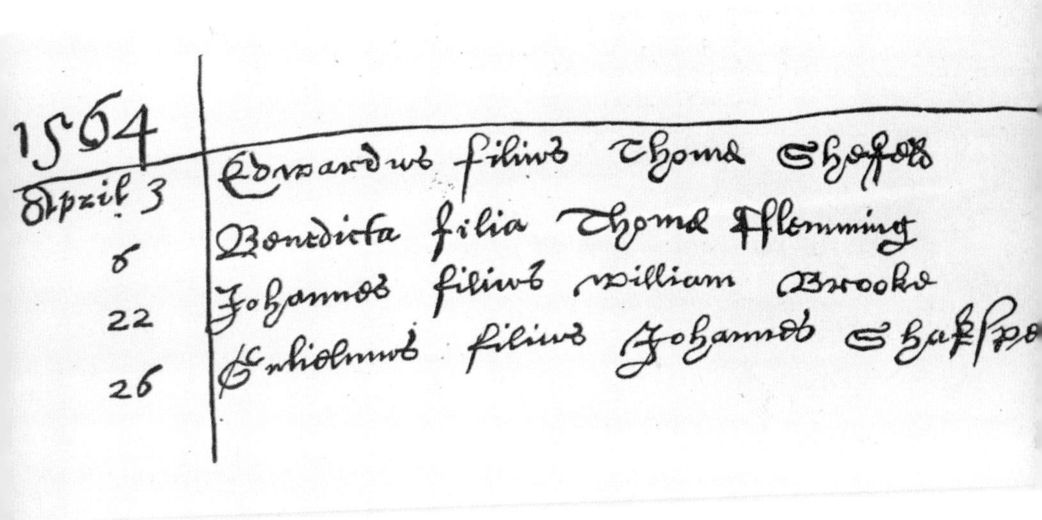

England in parish registers. Records of Catholics, many non-conformists, Jews and people of other faiths (of which there were comparatively few) were, for fairly obvious reasons, not recorded by the established church.

Parish registers date from 1538, although many of the very early ones have not survived. The registers were maintained by each parish and were normally in the care of the local vicar. In most cases baptisms, rather than births and burials, rather than deaths, were recorded. The records were maintained in a variety of ways and details were often somewhat sparse: For example, in the case of baptisms, the mother's name was not always given, while in the case of burials you will not always find the age of the deceased. If you are lucky, however, you may find such details and you may even find a note of the father's occupation and place of residence contained within the entries for baptisms. For marriages, you

ABOVE The baptismal register of Stratford Parish Church, with an entry for English playwright William Shakespeare on 26th April 1564.

LEFT A wealthy middle class Victorian wedding party parade in their finery.

RIGHT A Village Burial depicting a minister presiding over a funeral in a rural setting, mid 19th century.

may find the names of witnesses – who could well have been relations of the happy couple.

In many cases separate registers were kept for baptisms, marriages and burials, whilst sometimes the three types of events were recorded in a single volume. Things generally become a little easier from the mid-eighteenth century. After 1754 some registers contain pre-printed forms for marriages and this type of form was also produced for baptisms and burials from 1813.

Some parish records are still held by churches, but most have by now been handed over to County Record Offices. These county offices often have very helpful staff, especially if they know you are investigating your own family history. The County Record Offices also hold the records of post-1837 events but their indexing system is different from that of the General Record Office (GRO) so GRO Index references will not apply.

Phillimore's Atlas and Index of Parish Records can be of invaluable assistance when checking for pre-1837 parish records, as it lists the location of the records and notes

RIGHT Marriage records from 1834

where copies are available. However, you can always telephone the appropriate record office (or the one which you hope will prove to be appropriate) before undertaking what could prove to be a fruitless journey. If it turns out that the record you are looking for is still held within the parish, you may find that the local Vicar will make a small charge. If he or she doesn't, they will certainly accept a modest donation.

From 1754 until 1837, only Church of England baptisms and marriages had legal status, although Quakers and Jews were exempted from what seems today to be a most extraordinary law. Presumably, you could be buried, whatever your religion. Catholics and non-conformist Protestants thus suffered severe discrimination, even though there were many hundreds of thousands - possibly millions - of them. There were non-conformist chapels all over Britain and there continued to be a large number of Roman Catholic churches. The National Index of Parish Registers gives details of the whereabouts of non-conformist, Catholic and Jewish registers, while the National Archives also holds a number of Catholic registers and the registers earlier maintained by the Society of Friends (Quakers).

It sometimes happens that one is unable to find a record of the registration of a birth which occurred after 1837. As has been previously mentioned some births were not registered after this date, but the child may nevertheless have been Christened or Baptised: in such cases, it may be worth checking the parish records.

Manorial Records

Manorial records of various sorts were compiled from the Middle Ages onwards. They are sometimes hard to locate and they can be even harder to read, but in the absence of parish records they can tell you a lot. In fact, they will often tell you more about your ancestors than parish records and they are usually remarkably accurate.

The manors themselves came about during the Middle Ages and manorial documents record local court proceedings. The courts were attended by local people who could interrupt the proceedings if they felt mistakes were being made, or lies were being told. It all sounds remarkably democratic for the time.

Many manorial records deal with land, leases, tenancies and inheritance and, if you find your ancestors mentioned, provide you with a lot of background information concerning the way they lived and whether they were rich or poor. Boundary disputes or non-payment of rent quite often loom large. There is insufficient space in a book of this size to go into manorial records in any depth, but the Manorial Society of Great Britain and its website, is able to give valuable guidance.

The International Genealogical Index

The internet is mentioned frequently in this book, and there are many websites of use to family historians. New sites come along all the time and occasionally a site will disappear, but most of the really useful ones have now been around for quite a while.

For baptismal and marriage records before 1837 (but not for deaths or burials) one site stands out – Family Search, which is run by the Church of Jesus Christ of Latter Day Saints, otherwise known as the Mormons. Family Search has many parts and altogether lists more than 400 million names worldwide. As far as pre-1837 records are concerned, it is their International Genealogical Index (IGI)

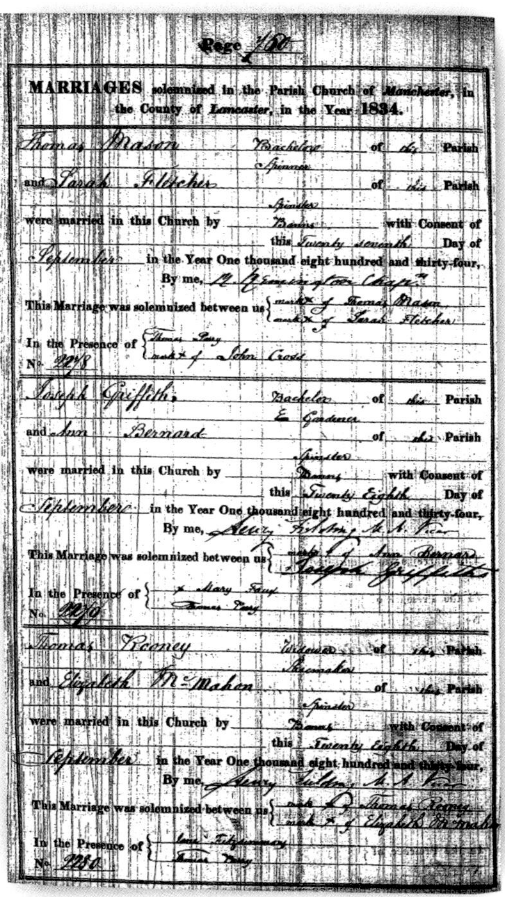

Page 160

MARRIAGES solemnized in the Parish Church of Manchester, in the County of Lancaster, in the Year 1834.

Thomas Mason Bachelor of this Parish
Spinner
and Sarah Fletcher of this Parish
Spinster
were married in this Church by Banns with Consent of
this Twenty seventh Day of
September in the Year One thousand eight hundred and thirty-four,
By me, [illegible]
This Marriage was solemnized between us { mark X of Thomas Mason / mark X of Sarah Fletcher
In the Presence of { Thomas Perry / mark X of John Cross
No 9248

Joseph Griffith Bachelor of this Parish
Gardener
and Ann Bernard of this Parish
Spinster
were married in this Church by Banns with Consent of
this Twenty Eighth Day of
September in the Year One thousand eight hundred and thirty-four,
By me, Henry Fielding M.A. Vicar
This Marriage was solemnized between us { mark X of Ann Bernard / Joseph Griffith
In the Presence of { X Mary Perry / Thomas Perry
No 9249

Thomas Rooney Widower of this Parish
Shoemaker
and Elizabeth McMahon of this Parish
Spinster
were married in this Church by Banns with Consent of
this Twenty Eighth Day of
September in the Year One thousand eight hundred and thirty-four,
By me, Henry Fielding M.A. Vicar
This Marriage was solemnized between us { mark X of Thomas Rooney / mark X of Elizabeth McMahon
In the Presence of { [illegible] / Thomas Perry
No 9250

which is probably of the most value. The index holds records taken from parish registers, as well as information supplied by members of the church based on their own research. The entries refer mainly to pre-1837 events, although there are some records from later dates.

LEFT A Victorian Christening ceremony with parents and god-parents at the baptism font

Good as the IGI is, it is far from being complete. Some parts of the country are sparsely covered and there are many errors, some of these clearly being mistakes made during the copying of the information and others being due to poor research on the part of some people who submitted information. The IGI is, however, very useful indeed – as long as you use the information as a starting point and do not take it at face value. It is also available on microfiche and CD-ROM, but the online version is generally more up to date. Family Search also maintains census indexes, an 'Ancestral File' and a 'Pedigree Resource File', all of which are free and well worth consulting. Mormon Family History Centres have the IGI on their own (mouseless) computers. The centres welcome visitors.

Obtaining Birth, Marriage and Death Certificates

Copies of England and Wales (post mid-1837) birth, marriage and death certificates can be obtained from the General Register Office (GRO) in a variety of ways. If you live in London or south-east England and you don't mind travelling to Islington, the place to go is the Family Records Centre (FRC). The centre houses an array of records, many of which are outlined in a subsequent chapter. For those starting out on their research and seeking to obtain copies of certificates, it is however the Indexes of Births, Marriages and Deaths which have supreme importance.

RIGHT In the vaults of Somerset House, 1966

Before you can place an order for a certificate, you need to find a reference to it in one of these indexes. The FRC has a large room devoted to the indexes of births, marriages and deaths and the whole business of consulting them can at first seem somewhat daunting. It is, however, quite easy, if a little tiring, once you get used to it. The indexes themselves are contained in large bound volumes, with red covers for births, green for marriages and, inevitably, black for

ABOVE Cartoon depicting an unhappy Victorian marriage

deaths. Each volume has a leather handle, to enable you to haul it from its shelf. The volumes are numbered and it is very important to replace the index in the correct place: there will be howls of anguish from other users if you don't! There are three separate sequences so, if you are looking for a birth, you need to head for the sequence of red volumes. Each year from September 1837 until December 1983 is divided into four quarters, as follows:

January - March
April - June
July - September
October - December

The entries within these volumes are arranged alphabetically, first by surname and then by first name. For most quarters, there is more than one volume, marked, for example, A-G, H-R, S-Z. From 1984, 'quarters' are abandoned and each volume contains a whole year of entries: this makes consultation a little less time consuming – although if you are searching for someone with a common name you will have to be even more careful than usual to make sure you have located the right person. There are an awful lot of John Smiths in each annual volume.

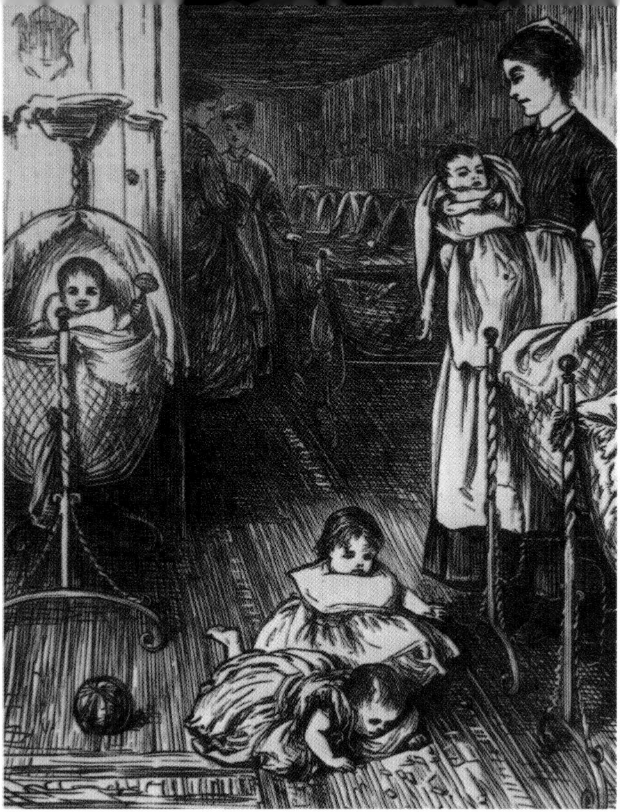

ABOVE Nannies take care of the infants at an institution for unwanted babies in Stepney, London.

Altogether, the FRC has something in the region of 5,000 volumes awaiting your perusal! And they are quite heavy. In fact, after a couple of hours, they become very heavy indeed. Some of the volumes contain copies of very old hand-written entries, but many have been typed and are easier to read. Nonetheless it is quite important to have some idea of the date of the event you are looking for. If you only know that a marriage took place within, say, a certain ten-year period, then you may have to look in as many as forty volumes before you find what you are looking for. Another thing to remember is that the event may not have been registered in the quarter during which it took place. This is particularly likely with births, as they were sometimes registered some months after the arrival of the baby.

BELOW A baptism in 1936

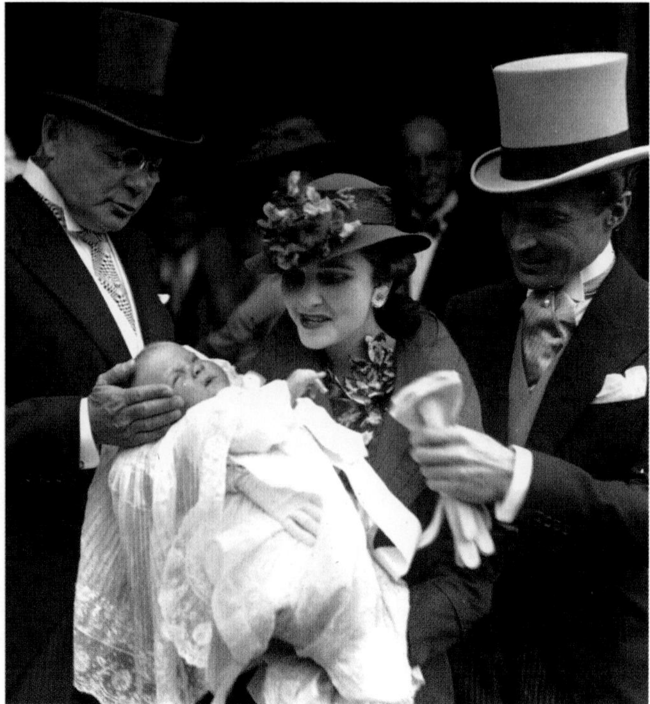

If you are just starting out on your research, you may well want to locate quite a few births, marriages and deaths at the FRC on a single visit. If this is so, it will save time if you look some of them up together. For example, if you are looking for the births of several children with the same surname and you don't know in which years they were born, it will be a good idea to check for all of them in each volume. However you organise your search, you will need to note which indexes you have consulted. It is remarkably easy to let your mind wander – and suddenly realise that you've forgotten which volume you've just looked at. This can happen if someone speaks to you, or otherwise offers a distraction. Some form of chart, which you can tick off, is a good idea. Failing that, always note any volume you may have missed, due to it being briefly (or not so briefly) consulted by someone else, so

ABOVE A Jewish bride signs a marriage certificate while the groom and other men watch

that you can return to it later. The indexes are heavily used, so occasionally a volume may be 'absent for repair'.

As well as the name of the person registered, each entry in the index contains the name of the district in which the event occurred, plus volume and page numbers.

Maps showing the location of Registration Districts appear on the walls and are also for sale in the shop.

The early birth indexes use Roman numerals and these can be a bit confusing at first. The volume and page numbers are, however, very important as,

RIGHT Gravestones in an English churchyard, 1857

without them, you will not be able to order a copy of the actual certificate. When ordering certificates from the Family Records Centre, you need to complete an order form, quoting these references and the year and quarter in which the event took place. Accuracy is important here, as a mistake in the references will mean that you won't get your certificate and you'll have wasted your money.

You take the form, plus a self addressed envelope (envelopes being provided at the FRC) to the counter and hand them in with the fee – currently £7 for each certificate ordered. The form is sent by the FRC to the General Record Office in Southport and your certificate(s) will be posted to you from there. This normally takes about a week, but it can take longer during busy periods. You can opt to collect the certificates from the FRC or, for the payment of an additional hefty fee, have them delivered to you within a day or so. Unless you have money to burn and you simply can't wait, this express delivery is seldom worthwhile.

The index entries themselves do not give you a great deal of information and you will very often wish to order a copy of the actual certificate. Even so, an entry

will confirm, for example, that great uncle Harry was born in Oldham in the first quarter of 1912 and this may be enough for you to be going on with. If you decide not to order a certificate, always note down the reference details, including the year and quarter, as you may later change your mind.

RIGHT A wedding group poses in the garden, 1900

The indexes for some later years do provide a little more information. In the case of births, the mother's maiden name is added from the September Quarter of 1911 (Aha! – so great uncle Harry's Mum's maiden name was Entwisle) while the death indexes, which do not show the age of death prior to the June Quarter of 1866, do give this information – from that quarter, until the April Quarter of 1969. After that, the date of birth is shown instead.

In the case of marriages, an important addition is the provision of the surname of the person married. This is shown from the March Quarter of 1912 and it can be very useful: You may not have known the name of the person's spouse, in which case the index has given you valuable information. You should also check the index under the spouse's name, both to discover his or her first name and to make sure that the reference numbers are identical. This is especially important with the more common surnames – it's surprising how many Smiths have married Browns!

The Family Record Centre is an important resource for those who are able to visit it, (see next chapter) but you do not have to go there to order copies of certificates. They can be obtained from local registration offices but, as their name implies, these offices are only able to provide copies of certificates relating to people who were born, married or died within the area concerned. You need therefore to be certain that you have journeyed to the right place.

FreeBMD

It is also possible to trace the events and to order certificates, online. Before ordering, you must of course get hold of the relevant reference details and there are two excellent websites which may enable you to do this. They are known as FreeBMD and 1837online.

FreeBMD is the one to try first because, as its name implies, it's free. It is an ongoing project aimed at transcribing the whole of the Civil Registration Index for England and Wales from 1837 to 1983 and makes the information freely available on its website. It is far from complete, as there are at present very few entries for post 1913 events and coverage of earlier years is not full either. In the case of

Births, coverage is a little patchy between 1837 and 1869, but from 1870 until 1909 (with the exception of 1881) it is very good indeed. The coverage of marriages is a little better: It is good from 1837 until 1852, patchy between 1853 and 1864 and excellent from 1865 until 1913. Death coverage is good between 1837 and 1852, patchy between 1853 and 1864 and excellent from 1865 until 1910. Of course, the coverage is improving all the time and the website allows you to see charts of the progress made to date so that you can judge whether or not you are likely to find the record you are looking for.

The instructions for searching the indexes of FreeBMD are quite easy to understand. You naturally need to know at least the surname of the person you are looking for and have some idea of the likely date of their birth, marriage or death. It also helps, particularly in the case of common surnames, if you know in which part of the country the event occurred. You do not necessarily have to be too specific, though. Indeed, being too specific can lead to failure to find an entry. You will fail to find the birth of the person you are looking for if you key in 'Kent' and they happen to have been born at Granny's house, just over the county border in Sussex.

In common with all transcribed records, the FreeBMD listings do contain a number of errors and some of these are mistakes in the spelling of surnames. Also, the spelling of surnames can change over the years: as an example, the name Hayward may be spelt Heyward, Haywood or Heywood – and originally it may well have been spelt Howard! In addition, one should never forget that many of our ancestors were illiterate. When registering a birth, a registrar might well have had to guess at the spelling, as the parents of the child may not have been sure how their surname was spelt. The answer is therefore to always keep your options open. Use the phonetic search facility if necessary and, where possible, move from the general to the specific.

LEFT 1837online.com

1837online

If you persevere with FreeBMD, you should find your ancestor – unless he or she happened to have been born, to have married or died in one of the periods not yet covered. If this does turn out to be the case, then there is always 1837online. This is an independently owned website which includes birth, marriage and death indexes from 1837 up until a year or two ago. It claims to be complete and it operates on a pay-per-view basis. It is obviously very useful for events not covered elsewhere.

You do, however, need to have some idea of the date of the event, as you will be charged for each quarter you view and this can turn out to be quite expensive. If you only need to look up one or two names and you have at least a rough idea of the date involved, it's worth going for the minimum payment (currently £5) for 50 'hits'. If you need to look up a lot of records, you can commit more money and the unit cost of each hit is reduced.

Online Ordering

Once you are certain you have located the correct index entries, copies of certificates may be ordered online from the GRO Certificate Ordering Service, with whom you will need to register. The online method is similar to the manual method one uses to apply for certificates at the FRC, with the same reference details needed and the same cost (currently £7 per certificate) involved. Make sure you have all the necessary details – otherwise the GRO will charge you a fortune!

What the Certificates Tell You

The birth, marriage and death certificates of your ancestors will give you a great deal of information. Although in more recent years they have appeared in a different format, all certificates bear the name of the registration district, the county or administrative area, the date of the event, the date it was reported and the name of the registrar.

RIGHT A birth certificate

Birth Certificates

Birth certificates are clearly very important, as they provide the place of birth, the name of the child, the name and surname of the father, the name and maiden name of the mother, the occupation of the father and the name of the person reporting the birth, as in this example:

When and Where born	Name, if any	Sex	Name and surname of father	Name, Surname and maiden surname of mother	Occupation of father	Description and residence of informant	When registered	Signature of registrar
First of March 1898 7 Heath Street Eccles	Hilda May	Female	Alfred Baldwin	Jane Baldwin, formally Entwisle	Journeyman Carpenter	Jane Baldwin Mother 7 Heath Street Eccles	Tenth March 1898	A.Child

OF AN ENTRY OF BIRTH

GIVEN AT THE GENERAL REGISTER OFFICE

Application Number B011397

N DISTRICT Eastry.

ub-district of Deal in the County of Kent.

2	3	4	5	6	7	8	9	10
Name, if any	Sex	Name and surname of father	Name, surname and maiden surname of mother	Occupation of father	Signature, description and residence of informant	When registered	Signature of registrar	Name entered after registration
...ily-...ne	Girl	Thomas Mason	Sarah Jane Mason formerly Frost	Private Royal Marines	Sarah Jane Mason Mother 9 North Sandy Lane Deal	Sixth September 1872	Thos. Placett Registrar	

opy of an entry in the certified copy of a Register of Births in the District above mentioned.

REGISTER OFFICE, under the Seal of the said Office, the 12th day of October 2000

1

CAUTION: THERE ARE OFFENCES RELATING TO FALSIFYING OR ALTERING A CERTIFICATE AND USING OR POSSESSING A FALSE CERTIFICATE ©CROWN COPYRIGHT

WARNING: A CERTIFICATE IS NOT EVIDENCE OF IDENTITY.

Z Series Dd 0541 250M 4/00 SP&SL(206688)

RIGHT A marriage certificate

It is worth noting that, during the nineteenth century, most babies were born at home, so it is likely that the address of the birth will be the same as that of the parent who registered it. It is also worth noting that, sometimes, no father's name appears on the certificate. This was normally the case when the mother was unmarried; the child was therefore illegitimate and registered with the mother's surname. Unmarried parents did, however, sometimes ignore this convention – see under Marriage Certificates below.

Another thing worth noting regarding births is that couples occasionally produced a child or two before they married. Having got used to the idea, they would then decide to tie the knot, the result being that the early children would be registered with the mother's surname while the later children would have their father's. In many cases, the earlier children would have been unaware that their birth certificate showed them to have their mother's surname so, when they married, they may well have called themselves by the surname of their father. Therefore, if you have failed to trace a particular birth certificate, it might be worth checking the index under the mother's maiden surname – just in case.

Births were normally registered within a few weeks of the event, although registration could take place much later. Birth certificates do not normally contain errors, although mistakes are always possible: second forenames or Christian names of parents are occasionally not recorded.

Marriage Certificates

Marriage certificates are often very informative. They give the date and place of the marriage, the names, ages and occupations of the bride and groom, the addresses of the bride and groom and, in

N ENTRY OF MARRIAGE

GIVEN AT THE GENERAL REGISTER OFFICE

Application Number **G011794**

emnized at the Parish Church in the Parish of St Mary Dover in the County of Kent

Name and Surname	Age	Condition	Rank or Profession	Residence at the time of Marriage	Father's Name and Surname	Rank or Profession of Father
bert London	22	Bachelor	Telegraph Clerk	Clarence Place	Edward London	Farmer
zabeth Ann Pain	21	Spinster		Clarence place	Thomas Pain	Professor of Languages

Church according to the Rites and Ceremonies of the Established Church, by - - - - ch after Banns by me, John Puckle

London
h Ann Pain } in the Presence of us, { H. Pain
Mary Underwood

n entry in the certified copy of a register of Marriages in the Registration District of **Dover**

FFICE, under the Seal of the said Office, the **11th** day of **August** **2000**

his certificate is issued in pursuance of section 65 of the Marriage Act 1949. Sub-section 3 of that section provides that any certified copy of an entry g to be sealed or stamped with the seal of the General Register Office shall be received as evidence of the marriage to which it relates without any further or of of the entry, and no certified copy purporting to have been given in the said Office shall be of any force or effect unless it is sealed or stamped as aforesaid.

ION: THERE ARE OFFENCES RELATING TO FALSIFYING OR ALTERING A CERTIFICATE AND USING OR POSSESSING A FALSE CERTIFICATE. ©CROWN COPYRIGHT

WARNING: A CERTIFICATE IS NOT EVIDENCE OF IDENTITY.

RIGHT The marriage certificate of Robert Browning and Elizabeth Barrett registered at St Marylebone Parish Church, London.1846

1846 Marriage solemnized at the Parish Church in the

No.	When Married.	Name and Surname.	Age.	Condition.
117	12th September 1846	Robert Browning Elizabeth Barrett Moulton Barrett	Of Full age	Bachel Spinst

Married in the Parish church according to the Rites and Ceren

This Marriage was solemnized between us, Robert Browning / Elizabeth Barrett Moulton Barrett — in Pre of

addition, the names and 'rank or profession' of the fathers of both parties. The names of the witnesses are also given: these are often family members but, even if this is not obviously the case, the names are well worth noting as the witnesses may well be later found to be connected to your family.

There are certain things to take into consideration when examining marriage certificates. The ages of the couple are normally given, but sometimes the words 'of full age' may appear. This normally means that the person (often the bride) was at least 21 years old, but did not wish to reveal her age. Alternatively, it may be that one or other party to the marriage was actually under 21 and was marrying without parental consent. Sometimes 'under age' will be shown for participants who were happy to admit they were under 21.

You are likely to find some interesting and strange-sounding occupations

…of St. Marylebone in the County of Middlesex

…ession.	Residence at the Time of Marriage.	Father's Name and Surname.	Rank or Profession of Father.
…"	Saint Paul Deptford.	Robt. Browning	Gentn.
—	St. Marylebone	Edwd. Barrett.	Gentn.

…blished Church, by Licence by me,

Thos. Woods Goodhawk Curate

amongst your ancestors. You may not be lucky enough to have a 'pure gatherer' (someone who collected dogs' excrement for use in the tanning industry) but you may well have a 'cordwainer' – a boot or shoemaker. A person's occupation may sometimes be misleading too, an example being a farm labourer describing himself as a farmer. While you are likely to have your share of agricultural labourers, you may also have a sprinkling of 'gentlemen'.

Gentlemen traditionally had private incomes and did not need to work for their living, but sometimes a middle class man would describe himself as a gentleman when he had retired from work with an annuity or pension. During the middle of the nineteenth century many 'gentlemen' fell upon hard times and were forced to get themselves a job for a while, perhaps as an unqualified solicitor or a clerk. They may then later have reverted to their gentlemanly status.

ABOVE People in a workhouse in the early 19th century

On nineteenth century and many twentieth century certificates the words Bachelor, Spinster, Widow or Widower normally appear under the heading 'Condition'. If one of the parties was divorced, then this will be shown, but it was hardly ever the case until comparatively recently. Before 1858, a divorce could only be obtained by a private Act of Parliament and was therefore virtually impossible to obtain. Even after that date, divorce was extremely expensive and, for many decades, it could be afforded only by the very rich. Besides this, there was a great deal of stigma attached to divorce proceedings: you would not be received by 'polite society' if your marriage had ended in this way.

In certain circumstances, however, it was possible for some people to obtain a Pauper's Divorce. If a woman left her husband and children and went off with someone else, then the husband might be able to get such an annulment. He would not be received by polite society, of course, but then again he probably wouldn't care too much – he would be too busy trying to earn a living and searching for a new wife who was willing and able to bring up his six children. In Scotland, divorce was a little easier to obtain provided adultery or desertion could be proved.

Because divorce was impossible for most people, bigamy was rife. It was a punishable offence, but that didn't stop thousands of people from doing it: They would simply move to another area, re-marry and hope they would not be found out. They seldom were, but one wonders how often the new spouse knew they were marrying someone who had uttered the marriage vows on a previous occasion. If this happened to a member of your family in the distant past, you may never discover whether they knew or not. It is however important to bear in mind that one of your ancestors may have married bigamously. He or she (it almost always seemed to be a 'he') will have declared themselves to be a bachelor or a spinster of course (or perhaps a widow or widower) and that may be the cause of some confusion in your research.

Official records and certificates of all kinds are prone to inaccuracy, but it seems that marriage certificates are particularly susceptible. There follows an example of information contained in a genuine marriage certificate, which contains no less than three 'errors'. The names and addresses have been changed (to protect the innocent!) but the details are otherwise as recorded on the certificate.

/hen arried	Name and Surname	Age	Condition	Rank or Profession	Residence at time of Marriage	Father's Name and Surname	Rank or Profession of Father
0th ept. 938	Edward George Ealham	31	Bachelow	Motor Driver	78 Chipstead St. Fulham SW6	Thomas Ealham	Labourer (Deceased)
	Mary Jayne Underwood	32	Spinster	Cook	183 Coniger Rd. Fulham SW6	Ralph Underwood (Deceased)	Electrical Engineer

In this case, both the bride and the groom happen to have been illegitimate. During the 1930s this was still considered to be somewhat shameful and few people liked to admit that their parents had not been married. Edward George Ealham's father was actually called George Downton, but Edward George had been registered with his mother's surname, which was Ealham. For the purpose of his marriage, Edward George opted to use his maternal grandfather's name of Thomas Ealham for the name of his father.

LEFT Women having their dinner at a workhouse in the early 20th century

Mary Jayne was in the same position – more or less. Her father was actually called Ralph Knott, but Ralph had not been married to her mother – one Mary Underwood. Mary Jayne decided to give her father's Christian name together with her mother's surname.

She did not have a copy of her own birth certificate, but naturally assumed she had been registered with her mother's surname of Underwood. Years later, when applying for a copy of her birth certificate in order to obtain a passport, she discovered that, after all, she had actually been registered with the surname Knott, even though her parents were not married. Ralph had clearly ignored the rules and pretended that he and Mary were actually married, so Mary Jayne need not after all have given false information – she could, quite correctly, have given her father's name as Ralph Knott.

The third error concerns the mortal state of Mary Jayne's father, Ralph. He had in fact left her mother many years earlier and Mary Jayne assumed that, by 1938, he was probably dead. In fact he was still very much alive and did not die until the 1950s.

To sum up then: Edward George Ealham's father was George Downton and not Thomas Ealham. Mary Jayne's father was Ralph Knott and not Ralph Underwood and Ralph was not 'deceased' at the time of the marriage. Had the family historian not known any of this when he or she obtained a copy of the certificate, then they would have been in severe difficulty, searching for marriages which never took place and a death which occurred much later than expected.

The moral of all this is that certificates should never be taken at face value. Always attempt to gather further evidence before drawing conclusions.

RIGHT A Death Certificate

Death Certificates

In general, death certificates are likely to provide a smaller amount of useful information than those for births and marriages. They do however give the date and place of death, the name, age and occupation of the deceased, the cause of death and the name of the person reporting the death, as in the following example:

When and Where died	Name, and surname	Sex	Age	Occupation	Cause of death	Description and residence of informant	When registered	Signature of registrar
Fifth December 1854 52 Derby St. Epsom	Thomas Pain	Male	64	School Master	Water on the chest	William Present at the death Epsom	Sixth December 1854	A Goodbody Resistrar

The 'informant' is very often the widow or widower of the deceased, or one of their children and quite often the relationship is noted on the certificate. This can be very handy, as you may discover a son or daughter of whose existence you were previously unaware. Occasionally, the full name of the deceased does not feature on the certificate. Anyone can report a death (it does not have to be a relative) and the registrar relies completely on the information given. So if the person reporting the death is not aware for example, that the dead one had a second Christian name and is not sure of their exact age, then these details will be missing or incorrect. Where the person reporting the death was illiterate and unable to write their name, the term 'The mark of...' will appear on the certificate.

Very often, the name of the doctor who certified the death also appears on death certificates. By the standards of today, medical science was in its infancy during the nineteenth and early part of the twentieth centuries. For this reason, the cause of

RTIFIED COPY OF AN ENTRY OF DEATH

GIVEN AT THE GENERAL REGISTER OFFICE

Application Number COL545141

REGISTRATION DISTRICT East Preston

922 DEATH in the Sub-district of Worthing in the County of West Sussex

1	2	3	4	5	6	7	8	9
When and where died	Name and surname	Sex	Age	Occupation	Cause of death	Signature, description and residence of informant	When registered	Signature of registrar
[T]wenty sixth [J]uly 1922 [4]5 Marine Parade Worthing U.D.	Arthur Percy Lee	male	32 years	Stockbroker's Clerk	(1) Lobar Pneumonia (2) Heart Failure Certified by A. S. Morton Palmer M.D.	Isabel Lee Widow of Deceased Present at the Death 45 Marine Parade Worthing	Twenty sixth July 1922	A. F. Linfield Registrar.

[CERT]IFIED to be a true copy of an entry in the certified copy of a Register of Deaths in the District above mentioned.

[Given] at the GENERAL REGISTER OFFICE, under the Seal of the said Office, the 16th day of February 2005

568712

See note overleaf

CAUTION: THERE ARE OFFENCES RELATING TO FALSIFYING OR ALTERING A CERTIFICATE AND USING OR POSSESSING A FALSE CERTIFICATE ©CROWN COPYRIGHT

WARNING: A CERTIFICATE IS NOT EVIDENCE OF IDENTITY.

TB

GENERAL REGISTER OFFICE ENGLAND

[D]X3 10/04 SPSL 009197

RIGHT A family are horrified to observe a white 'sheet' of wax winding from the candle.Superstition held this to represent the winding sheet in which corpses were wrapped

death often seems to be somewhat vague. Terms like 'senile decay' and simply 'old age' sometimes appear, but occasionally you will find a nice disease with a long Latin name, which you will have to look up in a medical dictionary. Much depended on the knowledge, or lack of knowledge, of the doctor concerned and sometimes on the social class of the deceased. It probably didn't seem worth finding out the actual cause of death of an 89 year-old farm labourer – in fact it's quite surprising that someone didn't simply give the cause of death as 'had a good innings'.

It may well be that one or more of your ancestors died (or was born) in a workhouse. Union Workhouses, as they were known, came into being following the 1834 Poor Law Amendment Act, the idea being to relieve parishes of the burden of caring for their poor via 'outdoor relief'. They were widely hated and regarded as a last resort for the poor and dispossessed but, as time went on, many of them effectively doubled up as hospitals for the poor. Sometimes, a widow or widower, having managed to stay out of the workhouse for much of their lives, would therefore end up dying in one.

Although workhouses are thought of mainly as nineteenth-century institutions, they were not finally abolished until the Poor Law was repealed in 1948, although by this time many had been officially converted into hospitals. During the 1940s a hospital at Oldham in Lancashire still contained a few of its old workhouse inmates. Caring people would leave items of food at the gates and the gatemen at nearby Oldham Athletic Football Club would sometimes let the old chaps enter the ground for nothing. One feels that this probably wouldn't happen today.

Other Resources at the Family Records Centre

The Family Records Centre in London is housed in a modern building and, as well as the indexes of birth, marriages and deaths referred to in a previous chapter, the centre contains a wealth of research material. The FRC is wonderful – but it can appear somewhat chaotic. Increased interest in family history research has meant that the centre has become very busy in recent years, although the advent of material available on the internet does seem to have led to a small decline in its popularity.

RIGHT The Family Records Centre

Researchers travel from all over the country to the FRC and they include people in coach parties organised by family history societies. Many who use the centre are well versed in genealogical research and know exactly what they are looking for and where to find it. Others are, quite understandably, a little more vague, but the professional staff are very helpful and will soon put you on the right track. The security staff are also very helpful and courteous: they don't like people smoking under the canopy just outside the building and will encourage you to move away but, in inclement weather, they have been known to offer an umbrella to a smoker who needed a break from his research.

Even non-smokers need a break, as things can get pretty hectic in the FRC. In the births, marriages and deaths section, there always seems to be a crowd of people surrounding the indexes in which you are particularly interested. The other rooms are less frenetic, but at busy periods it can still be hard to find a free microfilm reader or computer terminal. If you can, it's a good idea to remain beyond 5 p.m. on Tuesdays and Thursdays, when the centre is open until 7 p.m. It's much quieter then and you may avoid some of the rush-hour mayhem on the way home.

As well as the general birth, marriage and death indexes, the FRC holds, amongst other things:

- Records of Non-Conformist births, baptisms and burials (mainly pre-1837) and marriages (mainly pre-1754).
- Indexes of some births, marriages and deaths of British nationals and British Armed Forces, which took place abroad, from the late 18th Century. Records from both World Wars are included.
- Miscellaneous foreign returns of births, deaths and marriages from 1627 to 1960.
- Indexes of legal adoptions in England & Wales from 1927.
- Fleet Marriage Registers – registers of around 400,000 clandestine marriages which took place in London, often in prison chapels like the one at Fleet Prison,

The
Family Records
Centre
1 Myddelton Street
London EC1R 1UW
NATIONAL
STATISTICS
PUBLIC
RECORD
OFFICE
A service provided by
the Office for National Statistics and the Public Record Office

OPPOSITE The FRC building

- between 1667 and 1777.
- British Isles Vital Records Index on CD-ROM.
- Census Returns for England and Wales 1841-1901. The 1891 Census is available on microfilm and microfiche and the 1901 Census is available online. Full surname index to the 1881 Census, on CD-ROM and microfiche.
- Scot Link – online indexes to Scottish registration and census records.
- Family Search including the International Genealogical Index (IGI) on CD-ROM
- The 1992 edition of the IGI (British Isles) on microfiche.
- Death Duty Registers 1796-1858, and Indexes 1796-1906.
- Wills & Administrations from the Prerogative Court of Canterbury (PCC) 1383-1858 and associated indexes.
- Indexes to Wills & Administrations for the whole of England & Wales 1858-1943, on microfiche.

The FRC produces a number of leaflets describing the individual records and registers and telling you how to use them. There is a photocopying service and you can get free advice on family and local history research. The centre holds exhibitions, lectures and events and there are regular users' consultations as well as a quarterly newsletter.

The centre also houses a rather nice bookshop and information point where you can buy material to help you in your research and a family history reference area which includes books and maps. There is a baby changing room and facilities for the disabled. However, consultation of the birth, marriage and death indexes may cause difficulties for people with severe disability.

Finally, the Family Records Centre boasts a large refreshment area, where you may sit at small tables, eat your sandwiches and digest all the information you have uncovered. Try to avoid the one o'clock rush! The drinks machines are usually working (make sure you have plenty of loose change) but the sandwich machine often seems to be either empty or out of order. Take your own!

FRC – Current Hours of Opening:

Monday	9 a.m. to 5 p.m.
Tuesday	10 a.m. to 7 p.m.
Wednesday	9 a.m. to 5 p.m.
Thursday	9 a.m. to 7 p.m.
Friday	9 a.m. to 5 p.m.
Saturday	9.30 a.m. to 5 p.m.

(Closed on Public holidays)

Note: The London Metropolitan Archives building is situated just around the corner from the FRC and is well worth a visit if you wish to research ancestors who came from the London area.

Censuses

Census returns are invaluable to the family historian. Many people begin researching their family history by looking for births, marriages and deaths but, with the amount of census material now so easily available, it is very often a good idea to look at censuses first. A census return will probably give you a lot of detail, not only about the person or persons you are looking for, but also about other family members – some of whom you may not have known existed.

RIGHT A Hollerith machine for processing the results of the 1931 census

Censuses were originally conducted for statistical purposes, to measure population growth and demographic changes. At the beginning of the nineteenth century, with the population expanding, it was decided that, in the British Isles, a national census would be taken every ten years. Apart from the aborted census of 1941, which was not carried out due to World War Two, they have been taken ever

since. The first one to be undertaken on a national basis was in 1801. This and the censuses conducted in 1811, 1821 and 1831, were in most cases little more than headcounts, with hardly any details of individuals being recorded. They were presumably of some use to the government of the day but, with one or two localised exceptions, they are not generally of much use to the family historian.

For the purposes of the census, the registration districts and sub-districts were

RIGHT A man taking a census entry, 1871

divided into small enumeration districts. Then, as now, census forms were distributed in advance of census night. The local enumerator would collect them and enter the details in an enumeration book. In practice, because many people were illiterate, it was the enumerator who filled in quite a lot of the forms. The information contained within the enumeration books was later collated by clerks with blue pencils who marked the entries and sometimes made notes, thus making some of the information more difficult for us to read.

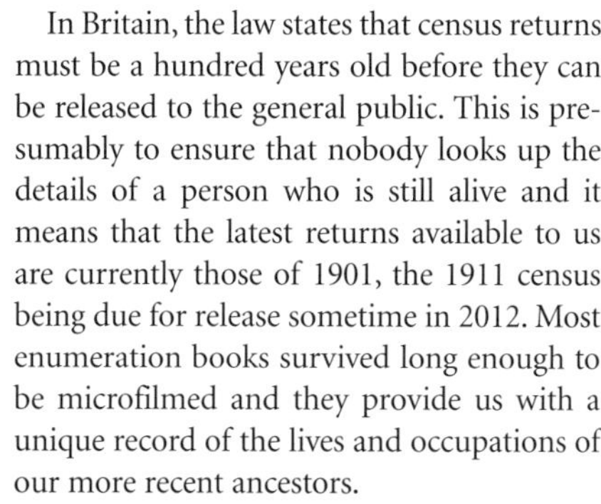

In Britain, the law states that census returns must be a hundred years old before they can be released to the general public. This is presumably to ensure that nobody looks up the details of a person who is still alive and it means that the latest returns available to us are currently those of 1901, the 1911 census being due for release sometime in 2012. Most enumeration books survived long enough to be microfilmed and they provide us with a unique record of the lives and occupations of our more recent ancestors.

During the nineteenth century, those in power wanted to know as much as possible about the population so that they could plan for the future. It is unlikely that anyone thought about the possibility of their descendants checking up on what they had told the census man many decades earlier and they would certainly not have envisaged amateur genealogists winding their way though rolls of microfilm, studying microfiche or looking up their details on a machine called a computer.

As with all historical listings, the census returns are not complete. Although most of the records have survived, not everyone was listed. Some people, for reasons of their own, were determined not to be located or counted and some were missed off accidentally. Masters and mistresses of households occasionally considered that the lower orders were not worth listing, so poor old Edith the scullery maid may have been omitted. When consulting census returns, it is also important to remember that the people listed were at the address in question on the night designated as Census Night. It did not have to be their permanent address, so if great aunt Hilda happened to be staying with her sister up the road on the night in question, she would be recorded at her sister's address.

1841

The census of 1841 is the earliest one to be of any real use to the family historian, as it has names, locations, approximate ages and occupations. Nonetheless, the details are fairly sparse: It seems that, as ever, people were suspicious of officialdom and it was not considered appropriate for the census enumerator to delve too deeply into people's affairs.

An 1841 census return has the following headings:

Place

Houses – 'occupied' or 'unoccupied'

Names 'of each Person who abode therein the preceding night.'

Age and Sex

Profession, Trade, Employment, or of Independent Means.

Where Born – 'Whether Born in the same County' and 'Whether Born in Scotland, Ireland, or Foreign Parts'

In the 1841 census, the address noted was often remarkably imprecise: sometimes simply the name of the village, or of the street, was recorded. As far as names were concerned, middle names or initials went unrecorded. Ages too were mainly imprecise: The ages of people under 16 were accurately recorded, but the census enumerators were told to round down the ages of everyone else to the nearest five years, so that, for example, someone aged 24 would be recorded as being 20. This seemingly bizarre instruction was thankfully ignored by a few enumerators, but this was Victorian England so most naturally did as they were told.

When studying one's family history, it is very important not to make assumptions. For example, in the census of 1841, no relationships are noted, so you may well assume that all the younger people in the household who bear the same surname are the children of the two recorded adults. This may not of course be so, as they could be nephews or nieces, or even grandchildren. The good news is that later censuses have a column for relationships.

1851 Onwards

From 1851, the returns contain additional and sometimes very useful, information. The 1851 headings are as follows:

Name of Street, Place, or Road and Name or No. of House

Name and Surname of each Person who abode in the house, on the Night of 30th March, 1851

Relation to Head of Family

Condition

Age of Males / Females

Rank, Profession, or Occupation

Where Born

Whether Blind, or Deaf-and-Dumb

List of the MEMBERS of this FAMILY, of VISITORS, of BOARDERS, and of SE
on the NIGHT of SUNDAY, APRIL 3

	(1) NAME and SURNAME.	(2) RELATION to Head of Family.	(3) CONDITION as to Marriage.	(4) AGE [Last Birthday] and SEX.		RANK, PROF
	No Persons ABSENT on the Night of Sunday, April 3rd, to be entered here, EXCEPT those who may be TRAVELLING or out at WORK during that night, and who RETURN HOME ON MONDAY, APRIL 4TH. Write after the Name of the Head of the Family the names of his Wife, Children, and other relatives; then Visitors, Boarders, and Servants.	State whether Head, or Wife, Son, Daughter, or other Relative, Visitor, Boarder, or Servant.	Write either "Married," "Widower," "Widow," or "Unmarried," opposite the Names of all Persons except Young Children.	Insert opposite each name the Ages of Males in Column headed "Males," and those of Females in Column headed "Females." For Infants under One Year, state the Age in Months, writing "Under 1 Month," "1 Month," "2 Months," &c.		Before fill… instru…
				MALES.	FEMALES.	
1	Charles William Augustus					
2	Clarence de Clere Smith					
3						
4						
5						
6						
7						
8						
9						
10						
11						
12						Govern…
13	my Family.	A Lodger	very nearly	Gent.		
14						
15						

I declare the foregoing to be a true Return, according to the

Witness

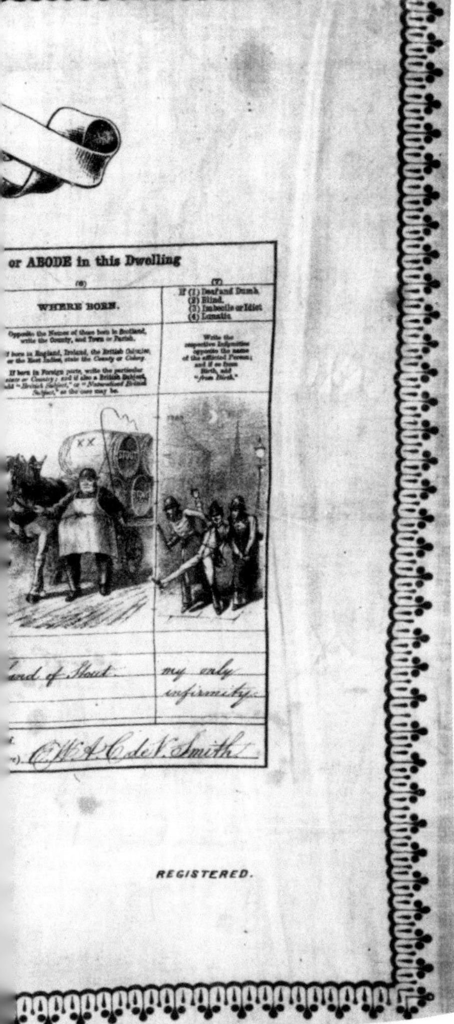
or ABODE in this Dwelling

WHERE BORN.	If (1) Deaf and Dumb (2) Blind (3) Imbecile or Idiot (4) Lunatic
[illegible]	[illegible]
...and of Stout	my only infirmity

...C. W. A. C. de V. Smith

REGISTERED.

LEFT A census form reproduced as a table mat, 1881

Under the heading 'Relation to Head of Family' you will normally find the head of the family, followed by the wife (if there was one) and any children. Other people may be described as 'Mother in law', 'Lodger', 'Visitor' or 'Servant'. 'Condition' indicates whether people were married, single or widowed. Under the heading 'Rank, Profession or Occupation' a woman might be described, for example, as 'Wife of a Farmer'. Failing that, she might simply merit a blank space – and be given no credit for her twenty-four hour a day role as housewife and the mother of half a dozen or more offspring. Children who attended school are referred to as 'Scholars'.

There are minor changes to the wording in 1861, but the returns are basically the same. In 1871 there are more minor changes, with the last column, instead of reading 'Whether Blind, or Deaf-and-Dumb' now reading: 'Whether 1 Deaf-and-Dumb 2 Blind 3 Imbecile or Idiot 4 Lunatic'

The 1881 returns are very similar to those of 1871, but there are some additions in 1891: These include columns for: 'Number of rooms occupied if less than five' and 'Employer, Employed or Neither Employer nor Employed'. In addition, Lunatics, Imbeciles and Idiots are all lumped into one category.

In 1901 there is a column for 'If Working at Home' and the 'feeble minded' are added to the column for the noting of disabilities. The Victorians clearly showed as little compassion for, or understanding of, the disabled, as they showed respect for the role of women. They wanted to know about those with disabilities, however, and the feeble minded had obviously slipped through the net during previous censuses.

Consulting Census Returns

Many local record offices and local history sections of public libraries hold microfilmed records of local censuses and some hold the records for an entire county. However, your ancestors are unlikely all to have lived in one small area, so you will want to search addresses in a variety of places.

LEFT An enumerator distrubuting National Register forms explains how to fill one in, 1939

There are many published census indexes and there are also many available online. You should normally start by consulting these, as they can save a lot of time and trouble. The 1851 census is particularly well covered by published indexes, many of which have been compiled by members of family history societies and other volunteers.

Of course it will depend upon when the people you are interested in were born or died, but a good census to begin with is usually that of 1881. The full 1881 census for England and Wales has been available on microfiche for many years and it can be consulted at, amongst other places, the Family Records Centre in London. The FRC also has 'finding aids' such as place-name indexes. The 1881 Census is available on the internet at the Family Search website, a free site which also has the 1880 U.S. Census and the 1881 Canadian Census. The Family Search people previously produced the 1881 census on microfiche. This is still available and should not be ignored as, in some ways, it is easier to use than the online version. It covers the whole of Great Britain and has full indexes by name, place of birth and census place.

There is in fact an increasing number of websites which will, usually for a fee, give you access to the returns from other years. Both Ancestry.com and Ancestry.co.uk are very useful in this respect, the latter having full England and

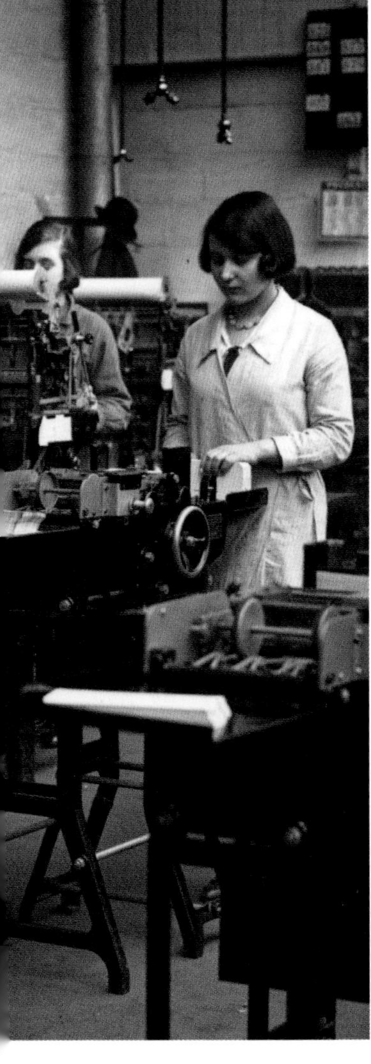

Wales census records for 1851, 1861, 1871, 1881, 1891 and 1901. Ancestry.com has many U.S. census records, as well as a lot of other databases. Registration is normally available on payment of an annual fee. Methods of consultation vary from site to site, but if you follow the on-screen instructions all will hopefully become clear. You are often able to download copies of the original census book entries.

LEFT Women at work in a factory manufacturing some of the machines to be used in the counting Britain's 1931 population census

When searching for births, marriages and deaths it is best not to be too specific when trying to trace someone in a census index. If you find too many possibilities you can always try narrowing your search. For the more unusual surnames always try alternative spellings and be careful with place names. When you do find your family, it's worth checking adjacent dwellings in case other family members were living nearby, as they often were.

Some census indexes will give you a lot of information and transcribed versions of the entries will, in theory, give you all the information you need. However, it is always best to view the original returns (on film, or via the internet) whenever possible. Transcribers, however well intentioned, frequently make mistakes and the

ABOVE Hundreds of women at work compiling information from the Census of April 1931

names of both people and places can easily be mis-transcribed. This seems to be particularly true of the 1901 census, which is available online from the National Archives.

The preparation work was largely carried out abroad, by people whose first language was not English and this inevitably led to numerous errors. It appears also to have led to parts of the 1901 census being lost forever, presumably in transit. The index to the online 1901 census is in many ways very poor. Many names, including place names, are wrongly spelt and this can easily lead you to consulting and paying for, transcribed records of the wrong people.

As well as errors made during transcription, there will of course be errors made at the time. The enumerator did not always obtain his information from the head of the household and his informant may have been someone who did not know, for example, exactly where some of the other inhabitants were born, or how old they were. Ages may be incorrect for other reasons: respondents would sometimes lie about their age for reasons of vanity, while the ages of young children were sometimes falsified in case someone noticed that an under-age child was working, perhaps in a cotton mill.

Very occasionally, a woman would describe herself as being a widow when she had actually been deserted by her husband. An example of this was a couple called William John and Mary Ann Frost. According to the 1851 census, they were both present on census night, but by 1861 Mary Ann was on her own and described as a widow. Miraculously, the 1871 census has Mary Ann once more living with husband William John, at the same address. He had come back from the dead or, more likely, he had simply come back.

This is a transcription of part of an 1891 census return which would also be confusing to the unwary:

Name	Relation	Condition	Age	Profession or Occupation	Where Born
Thomas Mason	Head	M	51	Gas Works Stoker	Cheshire, Stockport
Elizabeth do	Wife	M	46	Laundress Wash	Kent, Sholden
Fannie do	Daur in law	S	50	General Servant Domestic	do do
Charles Smith	Son in law	do	15	Farm Laborer	do do
Joseph do	do – do	do	12	Scholar	do Deal
Cecelia Mason	Daur	do	13	Nurse Maid	do do
Robert do	Son	do	10	Scholar	do do

Elizabeth Mason was the second wife of Thomas and two children by her first marriage formed part of the household. Although they are referred to as daughter in law and son in law, they were in fact Thomas's stepchildren. At the time, the term 'in law' was often used instead of stepchild. In addition there are three small errors: Fannie Mason was actually called Annie Smith, 'Cecelia' was actually spelt 'Cecilia' and Robert was actually Robert Crompton Mason. Apart from all that, the enumerator did very well! The poor chap (it was always a chap in those days) did of course have to rely on the information given to him on the doorstep and he would only write down what he was told. As far as the spelling of names was concerned, he may in some cases have been forced to hazard a guess.

In spite of the many traps and pitfalls, information from censuses can tell you a great deal, not only about your ancestors but also about the times in which they lived. And the information is relatively easy to find.

Wills

Wills developed in the Middle Ages, when there were strict rules concerning the inheritance of land and property. Under the Statute of Wills, passed as long ago as 1540, men aged 14 or more and women aged 12 or more were able to write Wills. By 1837 it seems that this was considered to be a little too young and so a new Wills Act raised the age for both sexes to 21.

RIGHT Draft copy of Scottish historical novelist Sir Walter Scott's will

Wills developed in the Middle Ages, when there were strict rules concerning the inheritance of land and property. Under the Statute of Wills, passed as long ago as 1540, men aged 14 or more and women aged 12 or more were able to write Wills. By 1837 it seems that this was considered to be a little too young and so a new Wills Act raised the age for both sexes to 21.

Wills have been held in public archives for centuries and for this reason the majority have survived. However, they have always had to be 'proved' by a court of some kind before they were given legal status and in order

ABOVE A Victorian family group

to avoid the cost of 'probate' some never got this far. Wills which have not beer proved may often be impossible to locate, although they may be held for many years by family solicitors.

In the good old days, Wills were of course hand-written. The writing is often ver neat and appealing – until you try reading it and you discover that you've taken o

a remarkably arduous task. The difficulties are compounded because, even when a person had comparatively little to leave, they were perfectly capable of writing a Will running to several pages. However, just like today, many people were not confident about the rules regarding the legality of Wills so, rather than write the thing themselves, they usually employed a lawyer of some sort to do the hard work for them. This probably accounts for the excessive length of some Wills and, again just like today, it must have been a nice little earner. The lawyers tended to use certain phrases which you soon become used to and the introductions are often fairly standard. All this can help you to decipher some of the later wording.

Many people left the making of a Will almost until the very last moment. 'Death bed' Wills were often dictated to a lawyer, who would then add his particular brand of legal language and ensure that the Will was correctly witnessed. Most poor people did not find it necessary to make a Will, as they had little or nothing to leave, but some did, so it is always worth checking. People who owned property usually

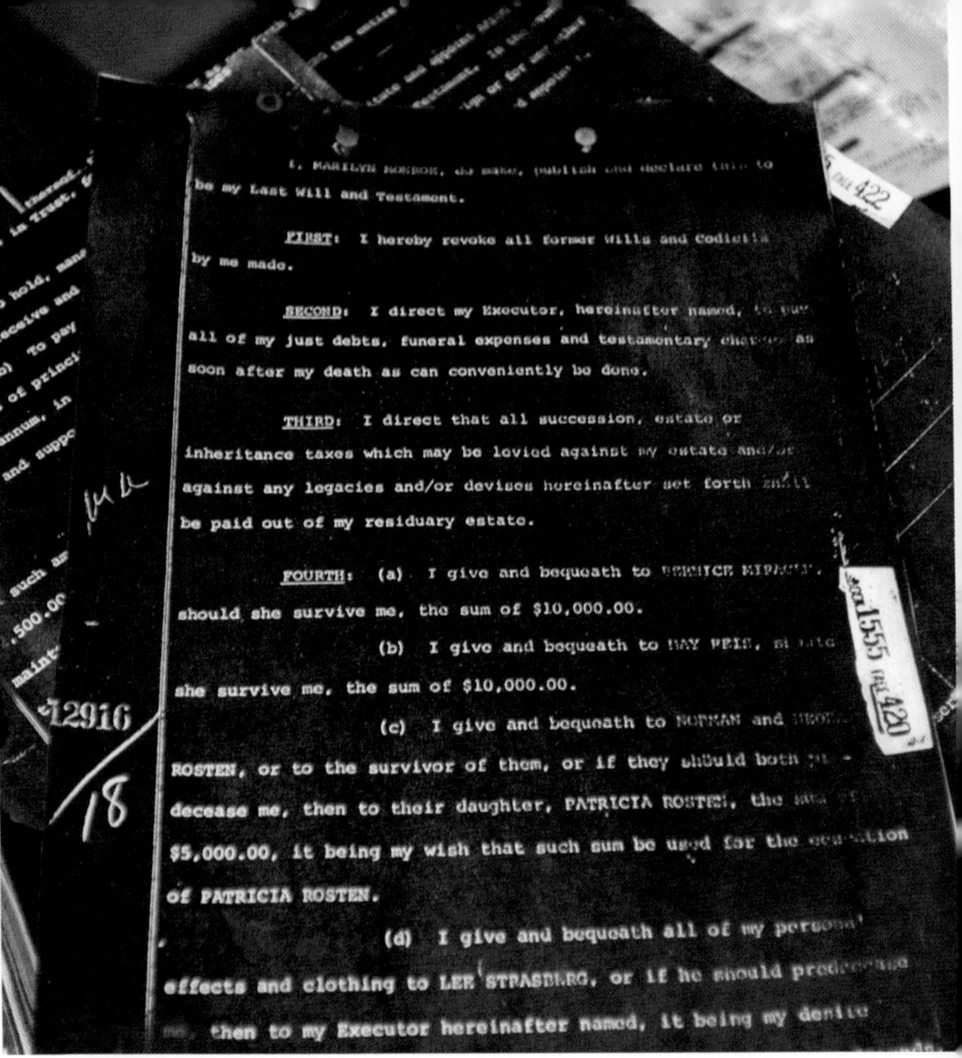

I, MARILYN MONROE, do make, publish and declare this to be my Last Will and Testament.

FIRST: I hereby revoke all former Wills and Codicils by me made.

SECOND: I direct my Executor, hereinafter named, to pay all of my just debts, funeral expenses and testamentary charges as soon after my death as can conveniently be done.

THIRD: I direct that all succession, estate or inheritance taxes which may be levied against my estate and/or against any legacies and/or devises hereinafter set forth shall be paid out of my residuary estate.

FOURTH: (a) I give and bequeath to BERNICE MIRACLE, should she survive me, the sum of $10,000.00.

(b) I give and bequeath to MAY REIS, should she survive me, the sum of $10,000.00.

(c) I give and bequeath to NORMAN and HEDDA ROSTEN, or to the survivor of them, or if they should both predecease me, then to their daughter, PATRICIA ROSTEN, the sum of $5,000.00, it being my wish that such sum be used for the education of PATRICIA ROSTEN.

(d) I give and bequeath all of my personal effects and clothing to LEE STRASBERG, or if he should predecease me, then to my Executor hereinafter named, it being my desire

did make one. If you are fortunate enough to find a relevant Will from the seventeenth century, it might begin something like this:

> *'I bequeath my soule to Almightie God (who gave it mee) and to Jesus Christe my onlie Savioure and redeemer by whose death and passion I fullie trust to have all my sinnes freelie forgiven and to attain to the joyfull resurrection of eternall life committing my bodie to the earth from whence it was taken to be buried in the Church of Chiddingstone...'*

Later Wills tended to use somewhat less flowery language, although 'Almightie God' would still often get more than a passing mention. Many early versions begin with the phrase 'In the Name of God, Amen' and feature such instructions as: 'My body to be buried in the Church of St. Mary at Leigh'. It was important that the person making the Will (the testator – or testatrix if a woman) could establish that he or she was 'of sound mind' in order to avoid the possibility of the Will being contested, so this phrase, or something like it, also frequently appears. The one thing always missing was any form of punctuation: commas and full stops are anathema to lawyers.

The various goods and chattels which testators left to people sometimes seem very strange today. In the seventeenth century Will noted above, William Woodgate left his son Andrew 'various goods including a bedstead with a canopy' while son John was to receive his 'grey colt'. His 'piebald mare and other goods' went to his married daughter, one Sarah Streatfeild. As well as valuable items, like brooches and rings, one also sometimes finds reference to items of kitchen equipment, such as pots, pans and wooden stools. Some of these legacies seem remarkably trivial, but they are of course very much of their time.

Wills are sometimes difficult to find, but they are well worth searching for. The amount of information they contain can be vast and include details of land and property owned by the testator. The majority of people did not own land, of course, but you may be able to work out someone's trade or profession from a Will and even the names of witnesses and executors may tell you something. Although early

LEFT A copy of Marilyn Monroe's last will and testament

Wills do not always mention, for example, the names of all of the testator's children, they sometimes do and this information may well fill gaps in your family tree. It is wise not to ignore any Wills made by people who are not your direct ancestors – your great great-grandfather's brother might have mentioned his nephew (your great grandfather) in his Will.

You will not find an old Will made by anyone who had been excommunicated,

LEFT Various funeral pyres

was in prison, or was deemed to be mad. Our ancestors had a thing about madness, perhaps because there was so much of it about. Spinsters and widows were allowed to write Wills – unless of course they had upset the Church, been thrown into prison or been 'committed'. They often did so, but prior to 1882, married women hardly ever made a Will, because they were not allowed to own anything. The Married Women's Property Act then came into being and was, in many ways, a first step towards emancipation.

When family historians are studying the Will of an ancestor, they are normally interested in two main aspects: Names and Money. Where money was left, it might be referred to as 'legal money of England' and quite often there does not seem to have been much of it. One could however buy a lot of pots and pans for a shilling (5p) in days gone by, so if someone was left, say, a Hundred Pounds, this was a fortune indeed. Very often, a rich landowner would also leave something like 'Five Shillings for the Relief of the Poor of the Parish'. Most generous. Still, it was better than nothing.

The Proving of Wills

Prior to 1858, the proving of Wills was mainly under the jurisdiction of courts administered by the Church. There were a great many of these courts, operating at various levels and they included Bishops' or Consistory Courts, courts administered by archdeacons and courts administered by bishops' commissaries or deputies. There were also some small areas which were exempt from the jurisdiction of the clergy, these being known as 'peculiar courts'. It was a remarkably complicated and indeed peculiar business but the final arbiter for England and Wales was often the Prerogative

RIGHT A church and its graveyard at Timperley in Cheshire

Court of Canterbury (PCC). The Prerogative Court of York (PCY) was usually the final arbiter in Wills made in the north of England.

From January 1858, church courts were replaced by a centralised system of civil probate registries. These Wills are now held at the Principal Registry of the Family Division in Holborn, London.

How and Where to Obtain Copies

For Wills proved before 1858, it is useful to know whereabouts in the country your ancestor died. There are many calendars and indexes available and the relevant county record office may be a good place to start searching. The Phillimore Atlas and Index outlines the different areas of jurisdiction, while Gibson and Churchill's Probate Jurisdictions: Where to look for Wills, is also a useful tool.

The website of the Federation of Family History Societies (FFHS) is well worth looking at and the National Archives website provides a number of databases online, including one for Wills proved before 1858. If you find the Will you are looking for on this site, you should be able to download a digital image of it for a small fee. Alternatively, you can have a copy posted to you. It's worth remembering that Wills were filed and indexed by the date of proving and not by the date of death: Sometimes a Will may not have been proved for many years after death, so you may need to keep looking.

LEFT A coffin is placed in a 200 year old horse drawn hearse

All pre-1858 Wills for Wales are held at the National Library of Wales and there is an index covering around 520,000 Scottish Wills from 1500 to 1875 at Scottish Documents.com. Scottish Wills are held at the National Archives of Scotland. Most pre-1922 Irish Wills have been destroyed, but fortunately quite a lot of them had previously been copied by local registries. The copies are held at the National Archives of Ireland, while those relating to what later became Northern Ireland are held at the Public Record Office of Northern Ireland. For Wills proved after 1858, indexes are held at the Principal Registry of the Family Division, which holds the original Wills (see above). They will conduct postal searches for a modest fee and copies of the originals are there to be had. You should, therefore, easily be able to discover how much money Auntie Agatha left to the cats' home.

Letters of Administration

When someone dies without making a Will, they are said to have died 'intestate'. Even today, many of us fail to make a Will, believing that our nearest and dearest will be able to sort out our affairs without too much trouble when we're gone. This may well be the case and usually a widow, widower, or other close relation can and could, apply to the courts for authority to sort out a relatively straightforward estate. In such cases, 'Letters of Administration' apply. The Letters of Administration become, like Wills, a part of public records and where no Will was made, they are worth finding. They normally tell you less about your ancestors than an actual Will, but they may nevertheless give you some information.

In 1818, one George London made a very long and detailed Will which took the author of this book many hours to transcribe (there are still a few words he can't make out). The Will gives a lot of information about property owned by Mr. London but, in this case, only one of his children is mentioned by name. Fortunately, when his wife Sally died some years later, many more names were listed in her Will. George London's Will begins as follows:

This is the last Will and testament of me George London of Tonbridge in the County of Kent yeoman made the thirty first day of October One thousand eight hundred and eighteen. I give and bequeath all my household furniture & farming Stock Crops Effects and property in and about my now dwelling house and the ffarm and lands thereto unto my wife Sally London for her own absolute use and benefit, also my will is that my said wife and my Brother Thomas London (whom I do hereby nominate and appoint Executors of this my will) shall carry on my business on the parsonage ffarm and Lands situate in the several parishes of Tonbridge as aforesaid and Leigh next Tonbridge until Michaelmas next and that all the Crops Stock and Property thereon be sold by them and the produce thereof and also the profits of the same ffarm...

The Will goes on to instruct the executors to take a bond from George's son 'ffrancis' for the payment of the amount of his share in the business of the Mill at Watt's Cross. There are frequent references to public stocks, ffunds and securities, cottages and lands adjoining the Turnpike Road between Tonbridge and London.

Basically, George left the lot to his widow Sally for her lifetime, with everything being divided amongst the children and grandchildren after her demise. If Sally re-married, then George decided that her 'interest in the guardianship of my said children and also in the executorship of this my Will shall immediately thereupon cease'. His brother, Thomas, would take over, alone.

The George London who made a Will in 1818 had a grandson, also called George. Young George's Will is much more concise than that of his grandfather and in many ways more like the kind of Will one might make today. It reads as follows:

This is the last Will and Testament of me George London Vicar of St George's Altrincham Cheshire. If my dear Wife Isabella London survives me, I give everything I have to her for her absolute use and benefit. If my said Wife should die before me then I give to my Son Herbert London my Policy of Assurance in the Church of England Assurance Institution for £700, the Silver Salver presented to me in 1873, the Skeleton Clock given to me by the late Charles Green of Savannah, the desk and writing table in my Study, the Bookcase in the Dining Room and all my books, except fifty volumes which my Daughter Beatrice may select at her pleasure. And as to the remainder of what I have I give everything to my Daughter Beatrice. Witness my hand this 17th day of January in the year 1888.

Signed by the Testator as his Will in the presence of us who in his presence at his request and in the presence of each other all present at the same time have hereunto set our names as witnesses Richd R Deane, Bank Clerk, Altrincham, Thos Fairhurst, Bank Manager, Altrincham.

Additional Resources

There are many other sources of information available to family historians and some of them are noted below. Although most of our ancestors may have lived ordinary, conventional lives and few were what would today be called 'celebrities', many of them still left their mark in one form or another.

RIGHT A grader at the British Museum Newspaper Library storing freshly processed negative film after being printed

Newspapers

Newspapers, both national and local, can be a valuable resource. Since the nineteenth century The Times, which began life in 1785 as the Daily Universal Register, has featured birth, marriage and death announcements within its pages. The working classes naturally could not afford to put a notice in The Times, nor would they have wished to, but in addition the paper always reported trials and bankruptcies, as well as events of general interest. If any of

obituary

SS M. CLASE, coupon checker, stol, died on 4 January, 1977. She red on 30 September, 1949, after years' service.

R D. S. INGRAM, clerk at ell/Lensbury Installation, died on January, 1977. He retired on 30 ne, 1953, after 24 years' service.

R. J. W. J. WALLINGTON, sistant movement controller at ndon Airport, died on 9 January, 77. He retired on 25 October, 1968, er ten years' service.

R. G. HUTCHINSON, section ad, Retail at North Central, anchester, died on 14 January, 77. He retired on 30 September, 75, after 23 years' service.

R. T. O. MITCHELL, senior clerk Sheffield Terminal, died on 18 nuary, 1977. He retired in 1967 ter 31 years' service.

R. F. A. COTTRELL, senior clerk S.O.&S.M. Division Office, died 17 January, 1977. He retired in 963 after 38 years' service.

IRS E. M. HAMMOND, ledger achine operator at Eastern ivisional Office, died on 18 January, 977. She retired in 1973 after 23 years

IR: L. V. CAESAR, clerk at unbridge Wells, died on 19 January, 977. He retired in 1951 after 30 ears' service.

MR. B. J. STRIBLING, operator 2 at Avonmouth Installation, died on 19 January, 1977. He retired in 1962 after 36 years' service.

MR P. OLLERENSHAW, driver, Eccles Installation, died on 20 January, 1977. He retired in 1958.

MR H. R. WATMOUGH, senior clerk, Stanlow Supply Depot, died on 14 January, 1977. He retired in 1965.

MR. A. J. CAVILL, airfield supervisor, Gatwick Airport, died on 11 November, 1976. He retired in 1963 after 34 years' service.

MR A. RAMSDEN, financial assistant, N. E. Regional Office, died on 23 January, 1977. He retired in 1967 after 35 years' service.

MR C. J. ELLIS, operator 1 at St. Leonard's Wharf, died on 23 January, 1977. He retired in 1967 after 42 years' service.

MR W. G. BURTON, clerk at London Divisional Office, died on 21 January, 1977. He retired in 1952 after 38 years' service.

MR. E. C. MASON, driver 1 at Lensbury Terminal, died on 26 January, 1977. He retired in 1966 after 33 years' service.

MR H. T. JONES, superintendent at Nottingham Depot, died on 24 January, 1977. He retired in 1955 after 27 years' service.

MR W. J. WILSON, estimator at Fulham M.R.C., died on 24 January, 1977. He retired in 1940.

MR E. S. MYCROFT, clerk at Southern Division, died on 21 January, 1977. He retired in 1951 after 21 years' service.

MR G. H. VERNON, driver at Power, Hanley Depot, died on 26 January, 1977. He retired in 1963.

MR R. C. B. LITTLE, driver at Stratford on Avon Depot, died on 29 January, 1977. He retired in 1948 after 17 years' service.

MR G. F. DOLLING, foreman welder at Fulham M.R.C., died on 31 January, 1977. He retired in 1962 after 43 years' service.

MR G. W. ALLEN, senior operations assistant at Fulham M.R.C., died on 3 February, 1977. He retired in 1972 after 25 years' service.

MR J. N. DALY, craftsman 1 at Fulham M.R.C., died on 2 February, 1977. He retired in 1974 after six years' service.

MR C. E. R. WAKEHAM, driver at Avonmouth Installation, died on 4 February, 1977. He retired in 1962 after 14 years' service.

MR S. A. D. SALTER, retail sales dev. rep at South West Region, died on 4 February, 1977. He retired in 1966 after 44 years' service.

MR J. LANKESTER, driver at Ipswich Depot, N.B.Co., died on 2 February, 1977. He retired in 1962 after 34 years' service.

MR D. GOULDING, driver at Brigg Depot, died on 2 February, 1977. He retired in 1950 after 31 years' service.

J. T. RODGERS, craftsman 2 at Fulham M.R.C., died on 7 February, 1977. He retired in 1974 after seven years' service.

MR A. SIMMONDS, driver at Penzance Depot, died on 2 February, 1977. He retired in 1954 after 32 years' service.

MR W. J. STODDART, labourer at Dingle Bank Installation, died on 6 February, 1977. He retired in 1957 after 19 years' service.

MR. F. COWBURN, operator 2 at Barton Terminal, died on 6 February, 1977. He retired in 1972 after 25 years' service.

MR A. TOTTON, motor inspector at Llandudno Terminal, died on 10 February, 1977. He retired in 1967 after 35 years' service.

MR E. KEATING, operator 2 at Purfleet Terminal, died 9 February, 1977. He retired in 1968 after 21 years' service.

BIRTHS.

On the 30th Nov., at Blenheim Palace, the CHURCHILL, prematurely, of a son.

On the 7th Oct., at Rangoon, the wife of HALKETT Lieut. and Adjutant 67th Regt., of a daughter.

On the 20th Oct., at Bombay, the wife of Capt. R.E., of a son.

On the 27th Oct., at Ranchi, Chota Nagpore, th NINIAN LOWIS, B.S.C., Assistant Commissioner, of

On the 6th Nov., 1874, at Belgaum, India, the wife M. PIGOTT, Esq., Lieut. 66th Regt., of a daughter.

On the 20th Nov., at Marlborough-terrace, Roath, of THOMAS J. ALLEN, of a daughter.

On the 21st Nov., the wife of POYNTZ WRIGHT, daughter.

On the 22d Nov., at South-hill-park, Hampstead, the STRAUBE, of a son.

On the 26th Nov., at Wolfang, Queensland, Austr HENRY DE SATGÉ, Esq., of a son.

On the 27th Nov., at Wolverton House, Bucks, the R. HARRISON, Esq., of a daughter.

On the 28th Nov., at Eton College, the wife of ART Esq., of a daughter.

On the 28th Nov., at Churt Vicarage, near Farnh the Rev. A. B. ALEXANDER, of a daughter.

On the 29th Nov., at 31, Spencer-square, Ramsgate, GEO. HAWKINS, late of Brighton, of a son.

On the 29th Nov., at Kibworth Beauchamp, Leicest of THOMAS MACAULAY, Surgeon, of a daughter.

On the 29th Nov., at Nunthorpe Grove, York, Mrs. of a son

your ancestors were famous (or notorious) then other national newspapers may too have reported events in which they were involved but, in general, local papers are likely to be a much better bet.

Local newspapers have always reported births, marriages and deaths and, if someone was a local worthy, he may well have warranted a full-scale obituary. In the not so distant past, funerals were often reported in great detail, with long lists of the names of mourners appended. At the time, these were probably put in to fill up the space, as well as to ensure that everyone who attended the funeral bought a copy of the paper so they could see their names in print, but now they may give us a lot of useful information.

Most of us have probably had our names in the paper at some time or other!

ABOVE The births column of The Times newspaper showing, at the top, the announcement of the birth of British statesman Winston Churchill

ABOVE An Obituary page from a company magazine

ABOVE The reading room of the British Library in the mid 1800s

In many cases we may have been mentioned because we got married, or did something else which was entirely innocent but, just like our ancestors, we may have appeared in court on a minor charge and this may have merited a few lines in the 'local rag'. Perhaps your ancestor was done for pinching a loaf of bread when times were hard, in which case he may well have been sent to prison.

CD-ROM indexes of The Times are available at the Guildhall Library, where searches can be made under names and topics. Many public libraries hold back copies of The Times on film or fiche and they also hold local newspapers in abundance, sometimes also on microfilm. Librarians are generally a helpful lot and Local History Librarians are particularly so. The British Library Newspaper Library holds national and local newspapers for the whole of the British Isles.

In 1901, a local newspaper in Norwich featured this report:

At the conclusion of Evensong at Norwich Cathedral on Wednesday, the Brass was erected by the Dean and Chapter in memory of the late Mr. Henry William Alden. Inscribed upon it in Church Text with Gothic capitals, is the inscription –
To the Memory of Henry William Alden,
who died from the effects of an accident December 26th 1901,
Aged 73 Years.
In recognition of 41 years faithful service successively as Lay Clerk, Master of the Choir School and Sub-Sacrist in the Cathedral Church.
This tablet is erected by the Dean and Chapter.

The descendant of Mr Alden, who came upon this report, was intrigued by the 'accident'. She obtained a copy of his death certificate and found that he died as a result of 'being accidentally knocked down by a horse and cart'. Nothing too unusual about that in 1901, but she later discovered that Henry William Alden, a widower, had re-married just three days prior to his unfortunate accident. It is a little late for police investigations, but Mr. Alden's descendant is still wondering whether his new wife was with him at the time of the accident. Did he fall – or was he pushed?

RIGHT Jesus College, Cambridge, 1955

Schools, Universities and Work

You may find old school reports amongst family papers, although if your ancestor was not academically bright he or she will probably have thrown them away in disgust years ago. The author of this book certainly did. If you do, however, know the name of a school attended by a forebear, it may be worth contacting, as school registers and other archive material could have survived.

Obviously, the records of public schools stand a much better chance of survival than do those of more modest establishments. When the author was researching his great uncle, one Henry Alfred Woodgate, he came upon the following entry, relating to Henry Alfred's attendance at the Christ's Hospital (Bluecoat) School:

Henry Alfred Woodgate: Clothed, aged 10, on 6th

LEFT Magdalen College, Oxford, 1934

October 1875. Presentation Papers dated 28th March 1875… Discharged from the school by his stepfather, Thomas Henry Heyward, residing at Thornbush Villa, Bensham Manor Road, New Thornton Heath, on 19th December 1879.

The circumstances of the discharge being that Thomas Henry Heyward has obtained him a situation in the Office of Messrs Tyser and Balme of 140 Fenchurch Street, Auctioneers.

This information threw light on Henry Alfred's subsequent career and it contained the bonus of providing his home address at the time he left the school in order to become an auctioneer's clerk. Together with information gleaned from other sources, all this confirmed that the Heywards were somewhat strapped for cash at the time.

In the twenty-first century we seem to have hundreds of universities, some of which appear to be willing to take in anyone as long as they can write their name. It was very different in the nineteenth century, when Oxford and Cambridge and later Durham and London, were the only options open to anyone. Of course, they were not open to many, but if you happen to have a Victorian clergyman in your tree, then he probably went up to either Oxford or Cambridge. Fortunately, all the older universities have archivists and they will be happy to help with your research.

If your ancestor was indeed a clergyman, then try consulting Crockford's Clerical Directory, which has been published regularly by the Oxford

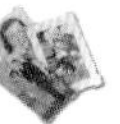

University Press since 1858. Records relating to, amongst others, service personnel, the police and civil servants, will be found in the National Archives at Kew. If you believe someone was probably a member of a trade union, then try contacting the local branch of the union concerned, as it may still hold records of former members. Failing that, the local record office may be able to help. For former members of the many professions, you can also contact professional bodies and institutions and if

BELOW Voters queuing up at a polling station, 1936

your ancestor worked for a major company then he or she may have featured in a company magazine.

Electoral Registers and Poll Books

Electoral registers list everyone who was entitled to vote at the time and are therefore very useful for establishing who was living where, during a particular period.

Originally arranged alphabetically by people's names, the registers gradually changed to an alphabetical arrangement by streets within each electoral ward. In the United Kingdom, they were first compiled in 1832 and, with the exception of a few years during World Wars One and Two, they have been compiled annually ever since.

In the early days, only men were entitled to vote in parliamentary elections and then only if they met certain criteria. The qualifications were modified from time to time and by 1884 most adult men had the vote. By 1918 all men aged 21 or more, as well as female householders over 30, were entitled to vote and in 1928 women of 21 were similarly enfranchised. In 1971, the right to vote was extended

ABOVE A female voter goes to cast her vote in 1923

to 18 year olds.

Things were a little more liberal when it came to local elections, where property-owning women (and there were quite a few) could vote from 1869.

The British Library holds a complete set of electoral registers for the United Kingdom from 1947 and it also holds some earlier registers. The BL needs 48 hours' notice for pre-1984 registers, as many of the records are held off-site. In order to use the British Library, a reader's ticket is needed and identification is also required. The Guildhall Library also has a selection of registers, especially for the 1830s, while the National Archives of Scotland and the National Library of Wales also hold registers for their respective countries.

County record offices and major reference libraries will normally have registers covering their local areas and they may also hold poll books. Poll books can be of particular use to the family historian, as they list all those who voted (including women, in local elections) stating the name of the parish in which they lived and, remarkably, even telling you for whom they voted. Poll books were compiled from the early part of the eighteenth century and continued until the introduction of the secret ballot in 1872.

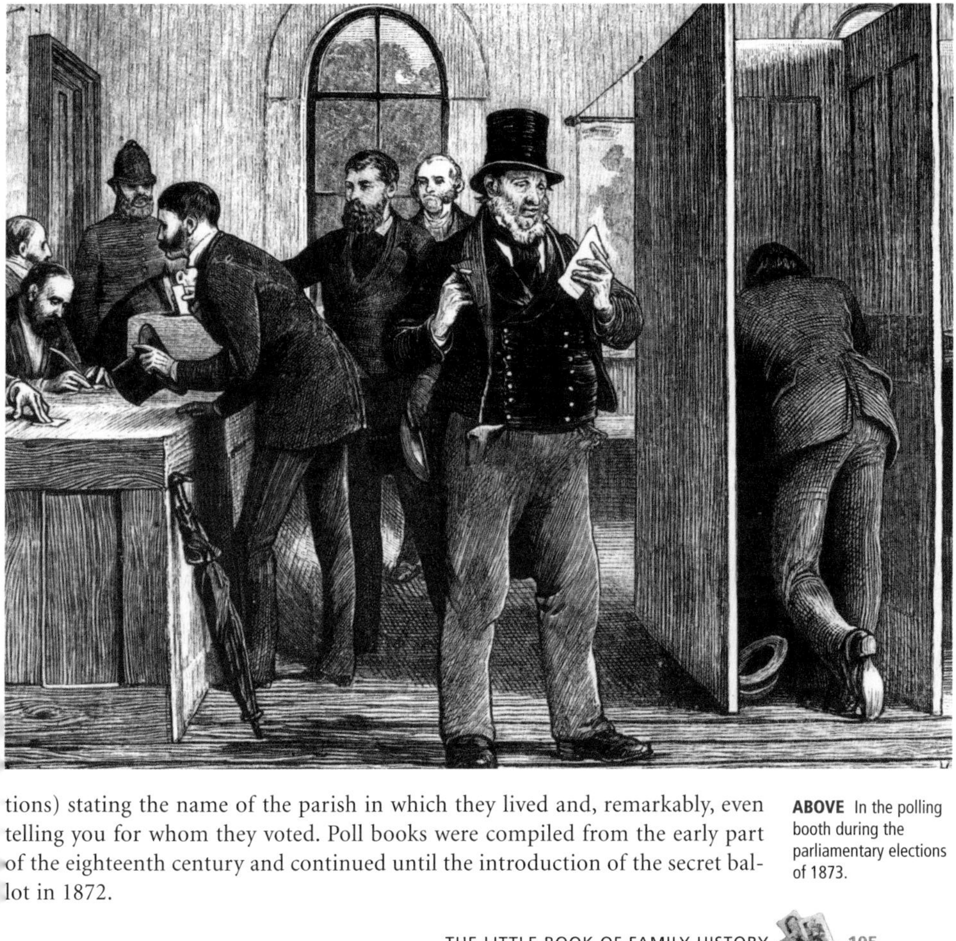

ABOVE In the polling booth during the parliamentary elections of 1873.

Directories

If you look hard enough, it is quite likely that you will find one or more of your ancestors listed in a directory of some kind. Directories mainly began appearing during the eighteenth century, with London starting to be covered annually from 1734 and other major cities following on in subsequent decades. By the early part of the nineteenth century, directories covering many parts of the U.K. started to appear. Most towns and many country areas were soon covered by one – and in some cases by more than one, as local firms would often fund their publication for advertising purposes. There were commercial, trades and street directories. Trades directories provided alphabetical lists of people arranged under the various trades, while street directories had residents listed on a street-by-street and house-by-house basis. Some also contained name indexes.

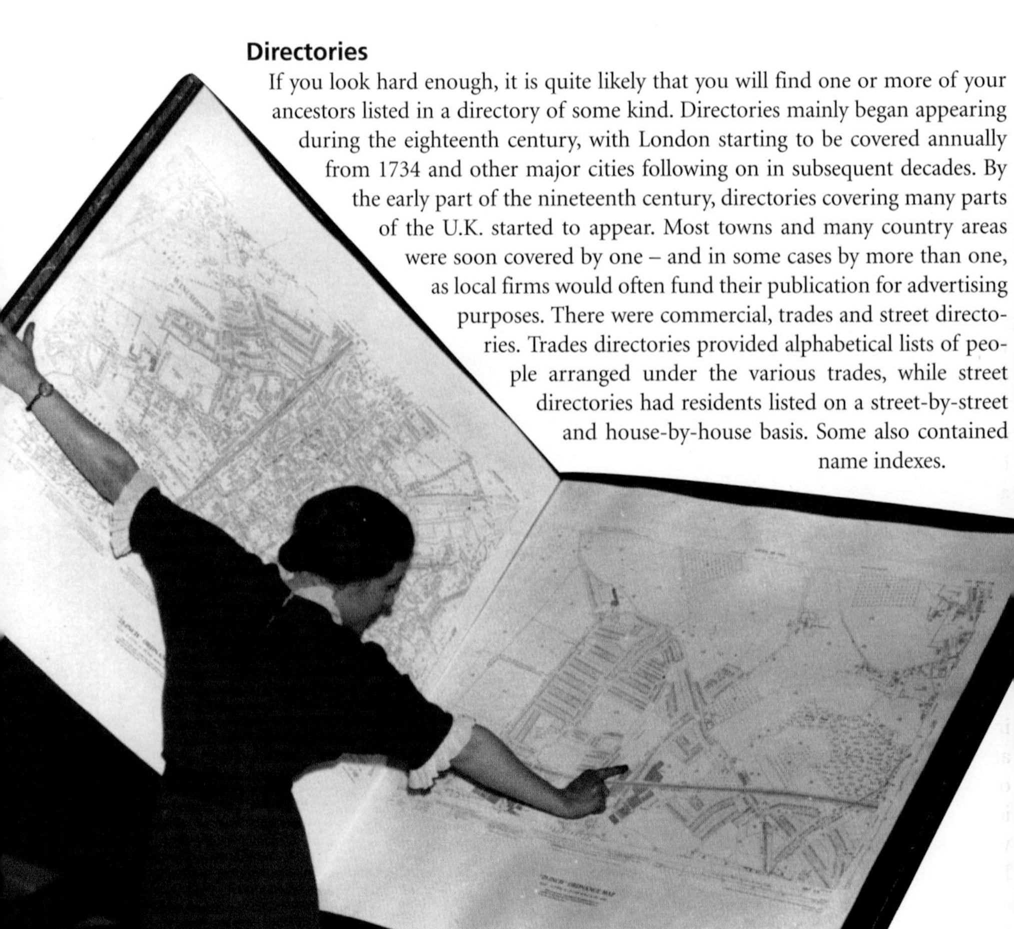

The earlier local directories mainly listed only well-to-do residents, with merchants, tradesman, clergymen and the landed gentry all getting a mention at the expense of the poor. Later, however, many local directories included all heads of households, whether they were well-to-do or not. Normally only the head of household would be listed, with wives and other residents not deemed worthy of mention.

Local directories usually feature advertisements for shops and services and they may tell you quite a lot about the area concerned. As with all aspects of family history research, these snippets of information should not be ignored, as they can provide clues which may lead you to discover all sorts of things concerning the lives of your forebears.

As with registers of electors, entries in directories can tell you where your ancestors were living at various periods in their lives and may tell you what they got up to over the years and give you an idea of when they may have died. You can then use this information in conjunction with birth, marriage and death certificates and census information. The Guildhall Library holds a large collection of directories but, if you know roughly where your ancestor lived, the best place to search is the local reference or local history library which, as well as holding a wide variety of directories, may have maps showing parish

ABOVE Yellow Pages telephone directory

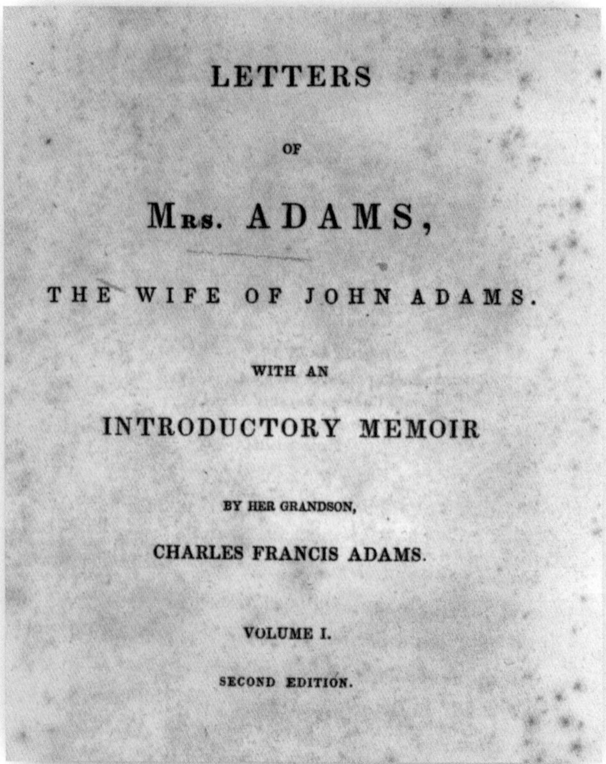

LETTERS

OF

MRS. ADAMS,

THE WIFE OF JOHN ADAMS.

WITH AN

INTRODUCTORY MEMOIR

BY HER GRANDSON,

CHARLES FRANCIS ADAMS.

VOLUME I.

SECOND EDITION.

ABOVE A book of letters written by Mrs Adams to her husband, mid 1840s

boundaries and will almost certainly hold Ordnance Survey maps.

Finally, don't forget telephone directories. These have been published since the end of the nineteenth century and, although most people were not 'on the phone' until about fifty years ago, there's always a chance that you will find someone listed at an earlier date.

Letters

The chances are that you will not find ancient letters in any family papers. All the same, if you happen to have any landed gentry amongst your ancestors, it may be that letters have been preserved in one form or another. In the introduction to this book, mention is made of elderly vicars from 'good families' undertaking genealogical research in times past. Sometimes they published the results of their labours. On the basis that few people would ever be likely to read these tomes and there was no money to be made from them by a commercial publisher, the books were often privately printed at the writer's expense. Luckily, copies of these volumes often survive and may be found in the local studies collections of public libraries. Here is an example of part of a letter, written by one Henry Woodgate to his father in 1780, which was reproduced in just such a volume:

Serjeants Inn, 12 Feby., 1780.

Dear Sir,

I shod think myself guilty of the most inexcusable neglect for not writing sooner, if I had not had particular Reasons for it. I knew it wod be expected of me to say something of Matrimony, & to tell you the Truth, I did not like to hazard an opinion without knowing how I shod like it, nor wod it have been at all the thing for so green and inexpert a Lad like me, three days after my Nuptials, to have talked loudly of the Joys and comforts of domestick Life & of the amiable Temper & gentle Disposition of my Spouse. But now having had time to look round the new Scene of Life, I have the pleasure to tell you in the sober Voice of Discretion that I never was half so happy a Man in my life, & I can assure you that if I had had my Wife on Tryal only I like her so well that I wod not exchange her for any other Woman alive.

And now, having said this much, let me not forget to thank you in the kindest manner for yr ready assistance & most generous support, which you lately so chearfully gave me. I know it is more than most Fathers wod have done, but then there are few Sons so happy in a Father as I am. We like our House, Servants &c. &c. very much, & have hitherto gone on very smoothly. I believe Mrs. W informed you that I had a Cow, which we find vastly convenient and advantageous; she supplies us with Cream, Custards, Syllabubs & yesterday for the first time we made three pounds of Butter......

I have had a very kind letter of congratulation from my Brother, but Mrs. Woodgate does not join with him in any of his good wishes, for her name is never mentioned. I have heard that she has said that she never will visit my Mrs. W as the slight of passing by without calling on her never can be forgotten. I sent a piece of Cake to my Uncle & wrote to him to make our Excuses for not calling on him, which he has since mentioned to sevl people and seemed much pleased with...

Mrs. Woodgate joins with me in kindest Love & best wishes, & I remain, Dr. Sir, yr most affectionate & dutiful Son

H. Woodgate

Two hundred and twenty-six years on, it's hard to know just what to say about this letter, other than that it is a wonderful piece of social history. Young Henry was clearly pleased with his new wife, but of course the document says much about the attitudes of the day and indeed about the class structure during the latter part of the eighteenth century. One hopes Henry continued to delight in the company of Mrs Woodgate, that his house and servants continued to please him and that his cream did not curdle.

Headstones and Memorials

Until the advent of cremation in the late nineteenth century, more or less everybody, unless they were lost at sea, ended up in a grave. They did not all get stone memorials of course: for many it was a simple wooden cross which will have long since rotted away, but many stone memorials have survived for centuries. If you know where your ancestor lived, then there is a good chance that you'll be able to find out where he or she was buried. This is especially true of rural parts, where people were often buried in a nearby churchyard. Matters may be more difficult in urban areas as, during the nineteenth century, many churchyards were beginning to fill up and cemeteries, some small, some very large indeed, began to be established.

BELOW American Military Cemetery at Madingley

County record offices will usually have details of burials in local cemeteries and the cemeteries themselves will often have their own records. Many parishes have transcriptions of the wording of headstones so, even where

ABOVE circa 1920: The British cemetery at Albert in the Somme

a stone is so worn as to be illegible, you may still be able to locate your ancestor's grave. At the very least, a headstone is likely to give you basic information such as the name, age and date of death of the person lying beneath the soil. With luck, it may also give you the names of children, as in the example below:

> **George London**
> died November the 20th 1818
> Aged 53 years
> Left 6 sons, 4 daughters viz
> Edward, Thomas Thatcher, Francis, Frederick, Samuel, John,
> Louise, Elizabeth Ann, Caroline Attwood, Emily

Some headstones also reveal a person's occupation, the name of their spouse and even the names of their other relatives. Information of this kind may also be found on memorial cards still in the possession of your living relatives.

Family graves are often grouped together, so you may well find other family members buried nearby. If your ancestor was killed in one of the two world wars and therefore buried abroad, then why not contact the Commonwealth War Graves Commission? Its website lists 1.7 million men and women who died between 1914 and 1921 (the official end of the Great War) and 1939 to1947. Should you visit a Commonwealth War Cemetery in France or Belgium, or one of the vast memorials to those with no known grave, you will not find very much in the way of detail. You will, however, undergo a very moving experience.

In Memory of John George
Son of George and Sally London
of this Parish who departed this life
March the 19th 1802
Aged 10 YEARS
My parents dear refrain from tears
I must lay here till Christ appears
Short was my time long be my rest
Christ took me when he thought it best

An example of a rather sad inscription, complete with a poem.

Forenames and Surnames

Forenames often run in families and they were frequently handed down from generation to generation. During the eighteenth and nineteenth centuries there were fewer names from which to choose, so every English family has its share of Thomases, Johns and Williams, as well as Marys, Anns and indeed Mary Anns. Just as today, children were often named in honour of popular or famous personalities of the time, fighting heroes and royalty being especially favoured in this respect. Fashion has always played its part in the naming of children.

The provision of a second Christian name was fairly uncommon amongst the working classes until Victorian times, when it became quite popular. It's as well that it did become more popular, as the provision of more than one forename makes accurate identification of our more recent ancestors that little bit easier. You are sometimes able to work out a family's religious denomination by the names given to their children – a girl called Theresa almost certainly being a Roman Catholic, a boy called Joshua perhaps coming from a Methodist or Baptist family.

Boys were very often named after their father and for a time, especially in the eighteenth and early nineteenth centuries, it was often the second son who was given his father's Christian name. And don't be surprised to find that a family had

ABOVE A Romany family at the back of their horse drawn caravan, 1926

LEFT The headstones of British soldiers killed in the 1944 D-Day invasion at the British military cemetery Bayeux, France. 2004

more than one child with the same forename: this sometimes happened when an earlier child died and a later one was given the same name. This can, of course, be the cause of some confusion to the family historian.

You may be particularly interested in the origins of names, in which case you will find there have been many books written on the subject. Many surnames derive from trades, so if you are called Carpenter the chances are that, somewhere along the line, you have an ancestor who was one. If surnames are a particular interest, you might like to join the Guild of One Name Studies, which organises seminars and conferences for members. It also publishes a list of registered surnames, which is available online.

If you would like to know whereabouts in the country a particular surname is likely to have come from, then University College London (UCL) has conducted research which is also available online. The website, called Spatial Literacy, features maps showing the distribution of surnames across Great Britain, in both 1881 and 1998. It will not tell you for certain where a family name came from, but it may give clues, especially regarding less common names. It is also very interesting to see how the distribution has changed between 1881 and 1998.

OPPOSITE A Romany woman selling wire baskets for preserving eggs.

RIGHT Families typically moved to the towns to work in the mills

Family History Societies

You would do well to join one or more family history societies. Obviously, if your family comes mainly from one geographical area, you may wish to join only the one relating to that area or county but, although people did not move around as much in days gone by, you still will probably find you have ancestors who lived in different parts of the country. In fact, people did move around more than one might think. It was not uncommon in the nineteenth century for families to migrate from the country to the burgeoning towns and cities, in order to get work and to enjoy a better standard of living. Whether their standard of living was actually better in the dark, satanic mills is, of course, another question.

Most counties and sometimes parts of counties, in England and Wales have a family history society and many of these now have a website. Naturally, the organisation and efficiency of the individual societies vary as they are run by volunteers, but the people concerned are invariably friendly and eager to help. Most societies organise talks and events of various kinds and, as these are nearly always interesting and quite often of a general nature, it may well be worth joining your local society, even if your ancestors come from elsewhere.

A typical family history society will produce a magazine or jour-

nal, often quarterly, featuring articles by members, news of branch meetings and updates of various kinds. There may be lists of members' interests, complete with postal and e-mail addresses, so that you are able to make contact with people researching the same names as yourself. There also exist 'specialist' family history societies, examples being the Romany and Traveller F.H.S. and the Anglo German F.H.S.

LEFT A Surrey Romany settlement in 1934

Membership of family history societies varies enormously but, as an example, the Kent Family History Society currently has more than 4,000 members, 17% of whom live overseas. It publishes a very well produced quarterly journal and as well as articles and lists of members' interests, it features News From the Kent Archives, Book Reviews, Letters and E-mails to the Editor, a noticeboard and offers of help with research. The society also produces and sells, microfiche of records taken from parish registers and other sources and, in common with many other family history societies, it maintains a library for the use of members.

You may also wish to join the Federation of Family History Societies. This organisation, a registered educational charity, was founded in 1974 and exists to co-ordinate and assist the work of societies or other bodies interested in family history, genealogy and heraldry. The federation has a publishing wing which to date has produced more than 170 titles. These include the National Burial Index for England and Wales, which covers much of the country but does not, as yet, cover much of London and south-east England. FFHS titles can be ordered via a separate website called GENfair. The FFHS also has another website called Family History On Line, which publishes online records compiled by family history societies.

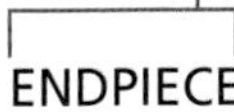

Endpiece

Once you have got going on researching your family history, you will almost certainly wish to take things further. You may even wish to join the Society of Genealogists and visit its library, which holds many books on local areas: in other words, places in which your ancestors may have lived. It holds dozens of county histories and thousands of family histories in book form, many of which contain family trees and pedigrees. Some of the family histories are, perhaps, not very well written, but that hardly matters. Members have also deposited research notes and there is a host of other material available for consultation.

If you wish to trace living relatives, then the Genes Reunited website may well be the place to visit. Started in May 2003, Genes Reunited is a spin-off from the Friends Reunited site. Its owners may have made a lot of money from it, but it is comparatively inexpensive to join and you may find it very worthwhile. You will need to put in quite a lot of your known family tree, including all those great aunts and uncles and then you will be able to make contact with others having the same ancestors in their trees. In the early stages, there will doubtless be many false hopes raised, as you'll find that someone else's Mary Ann Brown is not your Mary Ann Brown – even though she may have been born in the same area during the same period. However, in time, you are almost bound to locate a third cousin residing in Rutland or lurking in Lancashire and, when you do make contact with someone with whom you have some common ancestors, you may find they have information to add to your own discoveries.

You will probably also want to visit many of the websites already mentioned in this book, including Ancestry.com and Ancestry.co.uk They both contain a wide range of U.K. records, the latter including, as well as the census records mentioned elsewhere, United Kingdom and Ireland Parish and Probate Records, the England and Wales

LEFT A replica of one of the ships that Irish immigrants sailed in when they went to America to escape the potato famine

ABOVE A young Victorian man etches the name of his lover.

BMD Index, the Pallot Marriage Index (which mainly covers the London area) and Irish Immigrants – New York Port Arrival.

As you progress with your research, you are likely to become interested in some or all of the above. Parish registers have already been mentioned but as well as baptism, marriage and burial records, they also contain details of parish rates and minutes of meetings. These can throw much light on the nature of the parish concerned, as can settlement records, which relate to the arrival and departure of poor people who were claiming parish relief. In order to save money parishes were often keen to move such people on and the 'removal orders' may also be found within parish records. As ever, the local authorities were anxious to keep their costs down.

The author was once asked by his mother; 'Have you finished doing the family history yet?' The answer was, of course, that it is never finished and never can be. There is always more to discover and that is what makes it all so fascinating.

Appendix 1

USEFUL ADDRESSES, TELEPHONE NUMBERS AND WEBSITES

GENERAL

British Library
96 Euston Road
London NW1 2DB
Tel: 0870 444 1500
www.bl.uk

British Library Newspaper Library
Colindale Avenue
London NW9 5HE
Tel: 0207 412 7353
www.bl.uk/collections/newspapers.html

Church of Jesus Christ of Latter Day Saints (Mormons)
Family History Centre
64-68 Exhibition Road
London SW7 2PA
Tel: 0207 589 8561
Helpline Tel: 0207 384 2028

City of Westminster Archives Centre
10 St. Ann's Street
London SW1P 2DE
Tel: 0207 641 5180
www.westminster.gov.uk/archives

Commonwealth War Graves Commission
2 Marlow Road
Maidenhead
Berkshire SL6 7DX
Tel: 01628 634221
www.cwgc.org

Family Records Centre (FRC)
1 Myddleton Street
London EC1R 1UW
Tel: 0208 392 5300
www.familyrecords.gov.uk/frc

Federation of Family History Societies
PO Box 2425
Coventry CV5 6YX
www.ffhs.org.uk

Friends House Library (Quakers)
Euston Road
London NW1 2BJ
Tel: 0207 663 1135
www.quaker.org.uk/library

Guildhall Library
Aldermanbury
London EC2P 2EJ
Tel: 0207 7332 1862/3
http://ihr.sas.ac.uk/gh/

Guild of One Name Studies
14 Charterhouse Buildings
Goswell Road
London EC1M 7BA
Tel: 0800 011 2182
www.one-name.org

APPENDIX 1

London Metropolitan Archives
40 Northampton Road
London EC1R OHB
Tel: 0207 332 3820
www.cityoflondon.gov.uk/lma

Manorial Society of Great Britain
104 Kennington Road
London SE11 6RE
Tel: 0207 735 6633
www.msgb.co.uk

The National Archives (TNA)
Kew, Richmond,
Surrey TW9 4DU
Tel: 0208 876 3444
www.nationalarchives.gov.uk

The National Archives of Ireland
Bishop Street, Dublin 8, Ireland
Tel: +353 1 407 2300
www.nationalarchives.ie

National Archives of Scotland (NAS)
HM General Register House
2 Princes Street
Edinburgh EH1 3YY
Tel: 0131 535 1334
www.nas.gov.uk

National Library of Scotland
George IV Bridge
Edinburgh EH1 1EW
Tel: 0131 623 3700
www.nis.co.uk

National Library of Wales Aberystwyth
Ceredigion SY23 3BU
Tel: 01970 632800
www.ligc.org.uk

National Maritime Museum
Park Row
Greenwich
London SE10 9NF
Tel: 0208 312 6565
www.nmm.ac.uk

Principal Registry of the Family Division
First Avenue House
42-49 High Holborn
London WC1V 6NP
Tel: 0207 947 6000
www.courtservice.gov.uk

Public Record Office of Northern Ireland
66 Balmoral Avenue
Belfast BT9 6NY
Tel: 028 9025 5905
www.proni.gov.uk

Society of Genealogists
14 Charterhouse Buildings
Goswell Road
London EC1M 7BA
Tel: 0207 251 8799
www.sog.org.uk

REGISTER OFFICES

General Record Office
PO Box 2
Southport PR8 2JD
Tel: 0845 603 7788
www.gro.gov.uk

General Record Office, Ireland
Government Offices
Convent Road
Roscommon
Ireland
Tel: +353 (0) 90 6632900
www.groireland.ie

General Register Office,
Northern Ireland
Oxford House
49-55 Chichester Street
Belfast BT1 4HL

Tel: 028 9025 2000
www.groni.gov.uk

General Register Office for Scotland (GROS)
New Register House
3 West Register Street
Edinburgh EH1 3YT
Tel: 0131 314 4433
www.gro-scotland.gov.uk

Guernsey Register Office
The Greffe
Royal Court House
St. Peter Port
Guernsey GY1 2PB
Tel: 01481 725 277

Isle of Man Civil Registry
Deemsters Walk
Bucks Road
Douglas
Isle of Man IMI 3AR
Tel: 01624 687 039

Jersey General Registry
States Offices
10 Royal Square
St. Helier
Jersey, Channel Islands
Tel: 01534 502 335

SOME ADDITIONAL USEFUL WEBSITES

Ancestry.com A website containing many U.S. records.
www.ancestry.com

Ancestry.co.uk Has a wide range of U.K. records.
www.ancestry.co.uk.

B.B.C. Helps the beginner to get the most out of family history archives and has links to other websites.
www.bbc.uk/familyhistory

Census Online Links to online census records.
www.censusonline.com/links/England

Cyndi's List A list of genealogical sites on the internet, now having more than 270,000 links.
www.cydislist.com

Commonwealth War Graves Commission A free website which has details of First and Second World War deaths and the location of memorials.
www.cwgc.org

Cornish Census The 1871 Cornish census.
www.kindredkonnections.com

Family History Online Features online records submitted by family history societies.
www.familyhistoryonline.net

Family Search Includes, amongst other things, the International Genealogical Index and the 1881 Census Index.
www.familysearch.org

FreeBMD Free access to indexes of around 113 million births, marriages and deaths.
http://freebmd.rootsweb.com

Freecen A database for U.K. censuses 1841-1901. Still very incomplete.
www.freecen.org.uk

Genes Reunited Enables you to locate people with whom you share a part of your ancestry. *www.genesreunited.co.uk*

GENfair The online ordering service for the Federation of Family History Society's publications. *www.genfair.com*

Genuki A mass of information on U.K. and Ireland genealogy. *www.genuki.org.uk*

GRO Certificate Ordering Service The online birth, marriage and death certificate ordering service. *www.gro.gov.uk*

The National Archives Provides a number of databases online, including Wills to 1858 *www.nationalarchives.gov.uk*

Rootsweb.com Includes FreeBMD and FreeCEN. The oldest internet genealogy site. *www.rootsweb.com*

Scottish Censuses Access to the Scottish censuses of 1881, 1891 and 1901 *www.scotlandspeople.gov.uk*

Scottish Documents.com An index to more than half a million Scottish Wills and Testaments. www.scottishdocuments.com

University College London (UCL) Distribution of surnames across Great Britain. www.spatial-literacy.org/UCLnames
1837online An online index of births, marriages and deaths from 1837. *www.1837online.com*

1901 Census Now managed by Genes Reunited, but part of the National Archives. *www.1901censusonline.com*

Appendix 2

FURTHER READING

There are many books written to help you with family history research, many of which are published by the National Archives, the Public Record Office (PRO) or the Federation of Family History Societies (FFHS). Here are a few of them:

Tracing Your Family History
Anthony Adolph
(Collins, 2004)

Tracing Your Ancestors in the Public Record Office
A. Bevan (PRO, 2002)

The Genealogists' Internet
P. Christian
(National Archives, 2003)

Army Records for Family Historians
. Fowler & W. Spencer
(PRO 1998)

Probate Jurisdiction: Where to Look for Wills
J. Gibson & B. Langston
(FFHS, 2002)

Local Newspapers, 1750-1920
J. Gibson, B. Langston & B.W. Smith
(FFHS, 2002)

Wills and Other Probate Records: A Practical Guide to Researching Your Ancestors' Last Documents
K. Grannum & N. Taylor
(National Archives, 2004)

Tracing Your Irish Ancestors
J. Grenham
(Gill and Macmillan, 2000)

P.D.A. Harvey Manorial Records
(British Records Society, 2000)

Journeys in Family History
D. Hey
(National Archives, 2004)

How Our Ancestors Lived: A History of Life a Hundred Years Ago
D. Hey (PRO, 2002)

Making Use of the Census
S. Lumas (PRO, 2002)

Tracing Your Naval Ancestors
B. Pappalardo
(National Archives 2003)

Family Photographs, 1860 -1945
R. Pols (PRO, 2002)

Army Service Records of the First World War
W. Spencer (PRO, 2001)

Air Force Records for Family Historians
W. Spencer (PRO, 2000)

Other books also available:

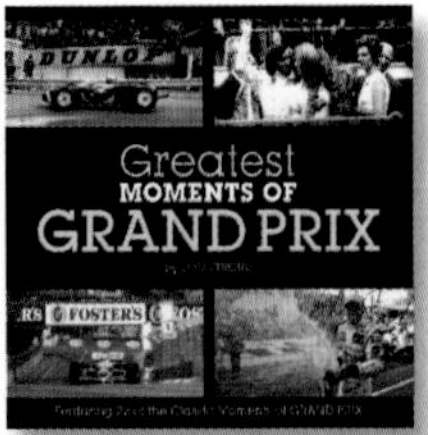

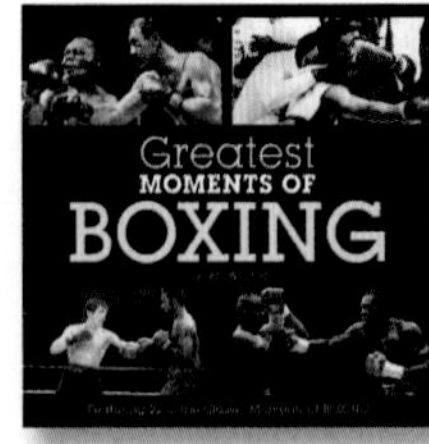

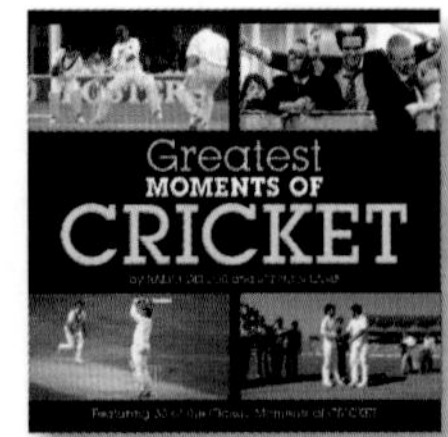

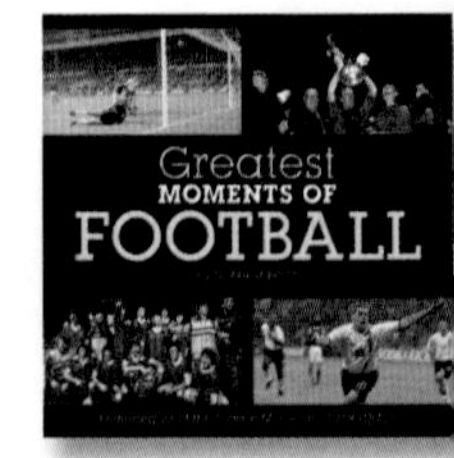

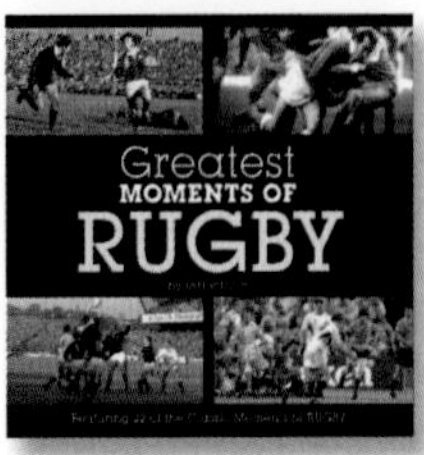

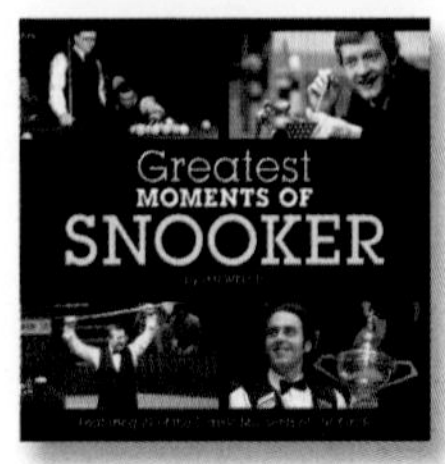

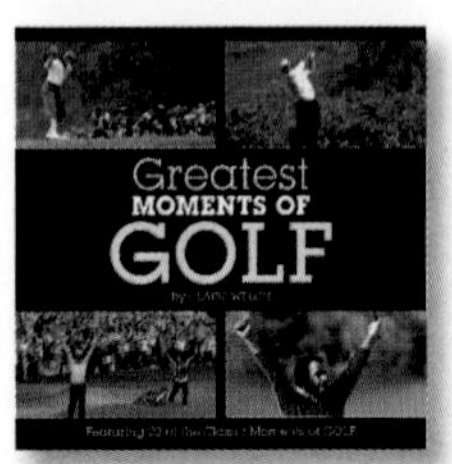

Available from all major stockists

The pictures in this book were provided courtesy of the following:

GETTY IMAGES
101 Bayham Street, London NW1 0AG

EMPICS
www.empics.com

Images supplied by Chris Mason

Creative Director Kevin Gardner

Published by Green Umbrella Publishing

Publishers Jules Gammond and Vanessa Gardner

Picture Researcher Ellie Charleston

Written by Chris Mason

This book is dedicated to the memory of Doris Isobel Mason, 1906-2006